THE HANDSHAKE

Ella Al-Shamahi is a National Geographic Explorer, palaeo-anthropologist, evolutionary biologist and stand-up comic. She has degrees in Genetics, Taxonomy and Biodiversity and is undertaking her PhD in Palaeoanthropology. She is also a TV presenter, a TED 2019 speaker and has taken four shows up to the Edinburgh Fringe Festival. For many years a fundamentalist Muslim, Ella practised 'handshake abstinence' with men until the age of twenty-six – these days she's a fan, although secretly she's more of a hugger.

THE HANDSHAKE

A Gripping History

ELLA AL-SHAMAHI

PROFILE BOOKS

This paperback edition published in 2021

First published in Great Britain in 2021 by
Profile Books Ltd
29 Cloth Fair
London
EC1A 7JQ

www.profilebooks.com

1 3 5 7 9 10 8 6 4 2

Typeset in Sabon by MacGuru Ltd
Printed and bound in Great Britain by
CPI Group (UK) Ltd, Croydon CR0 4YY

A CIP catalogue record for this book is available from the British Library.

ISBN 978 1 78816 781 9
eISBN 978 1 78283 837 1

For my favourite person, my nan – Halima (Margaret) Maflahi. You are the most incredible soul and truly the most generous. Here's to hugging you again soon.

Contents

Introduction

The handshake has a pretty serious PR problem. For a long time the go-to, multipurpose, international greeting, the handshake was abruptly banished in March 2020, as the COVID-19 pandemic swept the world. A common myth about the handshake suggests that it harks back to a time when you wanted to reassure someone that there was no weapon in your hand: the open palm, the shake up and down to dislodge any weapon up your sleeve, was a sign of safety and trust. But what if you can't see what is deadly? What if, to quote Gregory Poland of the Mayo Clinic, 'When you extend your hand, you're extending a bioweapon'?[1] Thanks to COVID, the underlying assumption of the handshake has suddenly been turned on its head. And even when it doesn't kill you, it doesn't exactly help foster connection and trust if the minute you touch someone's hand, you reach for the hand sanitiser.

Has the handshake gone forever? Is it consigned to history? Have we all been shocked into seeing what we should have realised all along: that it is sheer, reckless insanity to indiscriminately touch other people's dirty paws? The White House COVID-19 task-force member and immunologist turned American hero Dr Anthony Fauci certainly thought so, proclaiming that 'I don't think we should ever shake hands ever again, to be honest with you'.[2] You may think, if the handshake has been consigned to history – if it is indeed undergoing an extinction event – then who better than a palaeoanthropologist, someone who studies human evolution, to speak at the wake? Except that, as a palaeo-anthropologist … I'm refusing to write the obituary of the handshake.

Drawing on multiple lines of evidence, I have come to the conclusion that the handshake is in fact the owner of a rich, fascinating story, hiding in plain sight. See, I think the hand-shake isn't *just* cultural, it's biological, programmed into our DNA. The origins of the handshake go back far beyond antiquity, and probably beyond prehistory to before we were even a species. Our closest living relatives, the chimps, habitually use the handshake (it is more of a 'fingershake', really, which has many positive meanings, including 'let's make up'), indicating that hand-shaking probably began before our two species diverged – an astonishing 7 million years ago.

The handshake does, of course, have various meanings, both historically and geographically: we do the handshake a disservice to suggest that its only function throughout time has been as a greeting. Instead we should appreciate the handshake as a *unit of touch* (like a hug or kiss);[3] I believe we can't underestimate the importance of touch to the human condition, it is an innate impulse. Both psychologically valuable and comforting, the handshake is one of the gold standards of human connection.

Perhaps we always exist in a negotiation between our desire for touch and our fear of contagion, as an example from my own family reminds me. My father is *very* health-conscious and a tad compulsive about germs; when my younger brother was born he wrote out a sign in English and Arabic saying 'Please Do Not Kiss Me' and stuck it above the crib. He couldn't bear our massive family – and a plethora of visitors – kissing the new baby. We simply waited until Dad had left the room and … it was showtime. The kid was adorable (for a while, at least). But if at the moment we are more of my dad's way of thinking and – correctly – even fear the handshake,[4] the lesson of history is that we will tip back the other way as soon as it seems safe to do so. From the Black Death to the Spanish flu, the handshake has been banned, dropped and quarantined many times – and each time it has returned.

So I don't think the handshake died in March 2020 – rather, it's in temporary lockdown, social-distancing, quarantining, but, like most of us, going nowhere. Instead of being an obituary, this book is a tell-all biography, charting the twists and turns of the handshake's story through the lens of anthropology, cultural diversity, religion, history, sociology, biology, psychology, archaeology, gender and politics. Our prehistoric ancestors left handprints on cave walls, as if they wanted to reach through time towards us. The Greeks shook hands on the battlefield, and the Romans did so to mark marriages. The diplomatic handshake has shaped the destiny of millions, from ancient Mesopotamia to the lawn of the White House, while the handshake witnessed both the birth of democracy and its rise to prominence in the West hundreds of years later. Colonialism and globalisation have determined what *kind* of handshake we use (and there were and are plenty, including a penis handshake). Its history is littered with famous snubs, broken taboos, eccentric scientific experiments and national pride.

It's also deeply personal to me. I know the value of the handshake because I have lived with it *and* I have lived without it: for the first twenty-six years of my life – what I affectionately call my fundamentalist period – I followed strict Muslim law (in which the majority of Muslim jurists believe that men and women should not have any physical contact: no handshakes). It was awkward, and the tactics I adopted to avoid shaking men's hands in the UK in the noughties ranged from ingenious to ludicrous. (In fact, handshake dodgeball tactics weren't an unusual topic of conversation and humour amongst my fellow devout friends.) My Muslim background, it seems, was the dry run for social distancing; it was the Dominic Cummings going to Barnard Castle.[5]

Over the years I tried:

1. Avoidance: rarely works in a way which makes you feel good about yourself.
2. The right hand placed on the heart: I liked this as it made me seem mildly exotic, hippyish and it communicated warmth. I've found myself reverting back to this on COVID-19 Zoom calls.
3. A salute: I thought it made me look hip and cool. In hindsight, a Muslim woman in a floor-length, dark abaya cloak in the 2000s saluting people was probably startling and perhaps 'off-brand'.
4. Communication: I tried simply saying, 'Oh, I don't shake.' When delivered well it seemed endearing, but my delivery was often hit-and-miss – well, more hit-and-run.

5. Covering my hands with a glove or material: I decided that this was an acceptable loophole. However, I still cringe at the time I was handing over the keys of a Scout site to its manager, and, when he stretched out his arm, I quickly flicked my long sleeve down to cover my hand. I stuck to the rules! I was relieved, until my friend immediately commented on how unsubtle the whole thing was. I still worry that he might have thought that I didn't shake hands because I thought his were grubby. His hands were fine – I was just a bit fundo.

Very, very rarely I would relent. If it just seemed too awkward or if too much was at stake, I shook hands, and in doing so I was following a minority view amongst Muslim jurists that handshakes were permissible – as long as, and this was the important bit, they weren't flirtatious. I have since learnt that there is a big difference between hand-shaking and hand-holding.

As I became secular, I learnt to embrace the handshake. But there was still a protracted period of heightened awareness: touching male hands, with their strange sensation of coarser skin and larger size, was still very novel and I was hyper-conscious about all of it. Those with conservative religious views believed that when it came to touch, it was a slippery slope. They actually weren't wrong – at the time I was tentatively embracing handshakes, the secular world simultaneously wanted me to embrace the embrace. And hugs with the opposite gender were something I was *not* prepared for.

Although these days I am quite the hugger, at the time I

struggled with it: when my new best friend Rich tried to hug me, I would have neurotic conversations with myself along the lines of 'This is normal in this culture, this is just what people do, don't overthink it'. I basically had a mantra. A year or two later, when I confided this to Richard, he was, of course, mortified: he had had no idea what a culture shock it was. In a surprising plot twist, it turned out that Richard also hated hugs. He was forcing himself to do them because he thought it was just what people did.

At the same time, I was forging a career as an academic and explorer, specialising in hostile, remote and disputed territories. In one of my earliest *National Geographic* interviews, I was asked: 'What surprising thing is always in your field kit?' The answer was 'tonnes of disinfectant': even before COVID-19 emerged, I Dettol-ed toilet seats before using them and have been known, after a good hand-washing, to stand by the entrance of a public toilet till someone opens the door so I can avoid touching the handle. In some ways I had taken it too far, and in the field it was a bloody hassle. I found myself in a cave in a disputed territory being showered in dirt and bat guano. When it was time to eat, we didn't have any water, only antibacterial gel. All I was doing was wiping the mud, microbes and guano *around* my hand; at best, it was an exercise in redistribution. Enough was enough, and in January 2020 I made a promise to myself that I was going to care less about washing my hands. And I did. I guess a once-in-a-century pandemic is how the universe chose to repay me.

But even if it didn't quite turn out like I expected, I'm glad I overcame my fear of contamination, and I'm glad I learnt to shake, and that Rich and I persevered with our hugs. I'm happy that I normalised it all, because I can see how important physical contact is for human connection. The stricter Muslim law on this was specifically designed to create barriers against human connection between the genders, but now I cherish that easy bond between all humans. To be tactile, I would argue, is the best way to build a connection. Touch unites us in a way that keeping our distance can't bridge – ironically, an outstretched palm, a grip of someone else's flesh, is the physical embodiment of the hand on the heart. It's why the handshake, across time and space, symbolises so many positive things: agreement, affection, welcome, acceptance and equality. I've already lived through trying to find an alternative to the handshake – I'm telling you, nothing lives up to it. Some of us waited a long time to shake hands; I'm not ready to give it up.

1

Origin Story: Where Does the Handshake Come From?

Uncontacted

The Sentinelese live on North Sentinel Island in the Indian Ocean. Nominally it's a part of India, but in practice the people who live there govern themselves. The outside world knows almost nothing about them, and they know very little about the outside world; they are an 'uncontacted tribe'. In the age of globalisation this is no small feat; at a time in which most populations on earth are in contact with each other, where that contact is often instantaneous, where our societies and cultures grow ever more homogenous, uncontacted tribes are the dissenters. They have opted out. Having seen how 2020 played out, I'm inclined to commend them on their foresight. But their very isolation from this enormous information exchange that influences the rest of us means that they are fascinating for people who, like me, study anthropology and human behaviour.

The Sentinelese have a history of hostility to outsiders, which is entirely understandable, especially when you think that their most significant recorded contact with the outside world came when the British naval officer Maurice Vidal

Portman kidnapped a number of them in the nineteenth century. Some died immediately, probably due to a lack of immunity to outside infectious diseases, and the others were returned a few weeks later, presumably having been gruesomely experimented on, as was his modus operandi.

Before beginning the research for this book, I stumbled upon some extremely rare footage of the Sentinelese, taken in 1991 as the anthropologist Trilokinath Pandit and colleagues from the Anthropological Survey of India were cautiously trying to make contact. In the footage I watched, the anthropologists stayed in their boat and sent gifts of coconuts bobbing through the water towards the Sentinelese on the shore. Things were going significantly better than in other reported incidences in that no one had been shot by an arrow, and many of the Sentinelese were coming into the water to collect the coconuts. Then the narrator of the film explains that the Sentinelese have signalled to the anthropologists to leave. The narrator does not expand on this, but when I saw what happened, I almost fell off my seat. As a palaeoanthropologist I knew the implications of what I was looking at, and as a stand-up comic I was all too familiar with that sign – it was a favourite of some of my male stand-up buddies.

A tribesman had grabbed his naked penis and literally (not, figuratively, like my friends on stage) yanked his hand up and down it repeatedly. He was literally telling the anthropologists and cameraman to 'fuck off'. I recently saw a fellow cyclist in London use it to tell a driver this very same thing. But I had always imagined that it was a relatively modern gesture.

The implication was extraordinary: if people who are

uncontacted are doing something that is universally understood by those of us in the rest of the world, it strongly
implies that a sign or behaviour isn't a recent development.
Not because uncontacted people are 'primitive' or 'ancient':
they made it to 2021 just like the rest of us and are therefore
just as modern as we are. But their voluntary isolation gives
us an insight into a world before any kind of globalisation;
they didn't adopt their behaviour, traditions and manner-
isms from a popular sitcom or band, nor did their ancestors
adopt this behaviour from a missionary, an explorer or an
oil prospector. It is very possible that it is not 'learnt' at all,
but embedded in their DNA, the same DNA they share with
my furious British cyclist.

The Sentinelese made such an impression on me that
when I began writing about the handshake, my first question
was: do uncontacted tribes shake hands? The problem with
finding out is that first-contact encounters are incredibly
rare. Most are not recorded, and even if they are, they may
well be terrifying for the tribe – so we wouldn't really expect
the encounter to feature a polite 'How do you do, fancy
an Earl Grey tea and crumpets?' Yet, remarkably, evidence
exists for handshakes upon first contact with a number of
tribes. There is a *National Geographic* photograph, and
silent film footage, of a handshake that takes place in 1928
in New Guinea: it captures Ivan Champion, a member of
the 1928 US Sugar Expedition, with a man who is (presumably) a member of an uncontacted tribe, holding an oar in
his left hand and with his right hand shaking Champion's.[1]
David Attenborough tells a story about searching for birds
of paradise, also in New Guinea, in 1957, and getting into
a potentially hairy situation with a tribe who sound like

they might have been uncontacted. The whole incident was caught on camera. They charged at him while brandishing spears and knives and he averted the situation by simply sticking out his hand and wishing them a 'good afternoon'. They pumped his hand up and down.[2] I've faced neighbours in north London with less skill.

These handshakes are fascinating and, taken together, suggest that some uncontacted tribes intrinsically know what a handshake is without having previously come across one in the outside world – a remarkable finding. Of course, there are caveats: the hand-shaking may be behavioural mirroring (when people unconsciously imitate each other's behaviour and movements, often to build rapport), or perhaps the tribes weren't, in fact, uncontacted or had picked up this behaviour from other neighbouring indigenous groups who had contact with the outside world. However, the ethnologist Irenäus Eibl-Eibesfeldt describes encountering hand-shaking amongst tribes in New Guinea who had only made contact with the outside world some seven months earlier. The Kukukuku and Woitapmin tribes, as well as patrol officers, confirmed to him that they had always practised hand-shaking and that it didn't originate post-contact.[3] Additionally, there are reports of handshakes with newly contacted tribes in a completely different geographical location, the Amazon, in the 1970s. So we have similar reports from two different places: which also happen to be the two places in the world with the highest number of uncontacted tribes.

Did Neanderthals shake hands?

It was enough for this anthropologist to start thinking that the handshake might be much older than we were assuming. Popular origin stories for the handshake tend to mention the Quakers and medieval Europe, or – going back a bit further – the Romans, ancient Greeks and even Mesopotamians. Some do a disservice to the handshake (which is, in fact, as the stories above suggest, a truly international gesture) by suggesting that it was introduced across the world by Western missionaries. I think that starting at any of these points in time is akin to beginning a history of pop music at Justin Bieber; you missed a bit. But *how* old is the handshake? Would, say, our cousins the Neanderthals have shaken hands with each other – or even us? The presence of Neanderthal DNA in our own genomes is evidence that we certainly mated with them … so a handshake seems pretty banal by prehistoric inter-species standards.

Unsurprisingly, the archaeological and fossil records in this department leave a lot to be desired, and while rock and cave art do provide evidence of an obsession with hands on the part of *Homo sapiens*, nothing depicts an actual handshake in progress. And yet I would argue that the handshake is not just prehistoric, but that it has a deep evolutionary history: that it is older than our species and that, yes, the Neanderthals did shake hands. In fact, I would say the handshake is at least 7 *million years* old. How on earth can I be so cautiously confident even in the absence of hard archaeological or fossil evidence? Good old evolutionary biology.

If you and all your many siblings had ginger hair or blue eyes or, say, sickle cell anaemia, one might be forgiven for jumping to conclusions about the hair colour, eye colour and genetic mutations of your parents. But when we scale up from just looking at siblings and start exploring much bigger sections of the evolutionary tree, we start to get some fascinating insights into the DNA. Here's the thing: if a morphology or behaviour is exhibited in a few related species, we tend to assume that the last common ancestor of those species also exhibited that behaviour. (This isn't always true. Sometimes convergent evolution is at play, which is when evolution in different unrelated species converges to the same end result: for example, both birds and bats have wings they use for flight, but the former are technically dinosaurs and the latter are mammals.) Our closest living relatives are chimps (the common chimpanzee, *Pan troglodytes*) and their sister species the bonobos (the pygmy chimpanzee, *Pan paniscus*),[4] and, lo and behold, the primatologist Dr Cat Hobaiter was able to show that chimps and bonobos shake hands. These chimp and bonobo handshakes are typically really fingers overlapping: so 'finger-shaking' might be more accurate, though palm-overlapping has also been observed.[5]

And not just that: through painstaking observational work, Dr Hobaiter was able to show that the handshake was linked to a positive social interaction but that its precise function was quite flexible and hard to define, just as it is for humans today. It seemed to be deployed in various touchy-feely, friendly scenarios, as well as in greetings where there was a power imbalance, with the more senior-ranking individual sometimes offering a handshake as if to reassure and quieten the nerves of the lower-ranking individual. Remarkably, Hobaiter also describes two chimps fighting ferociously and then coming together to sheepishly shake hands: when

I spoke to her, she apologised for anthropomorphising, but said that she was struck by how similar it looked to two human teenagers begrudgingly shaking hands after a fight. And so, rather endearingly, it appears that the handshake is utilised by our closest living relatives post-conflict to mean 'let's make up'. The last common ancestor of chimps, bonobos and *Homo sapiens*, lived around 7 million years ago; it's reasonable to assume that not only did they shake hands, but so did all that ancestor's descendants – including the Neanderthals. In my informed opinion, the handshake is therefore … bloody old.

This is what we call phylogenetic evidence: phylogenetics is the study of evolutionary relationships, and a 'phylogenetic tree' is a tree representing that relationship, a bit like a family tree but on a very different scale. One wonders just how far back the handshake goes; might it even be older than 7 million years? Gorillas split from the lineage that gave rise to chimps, bonobos and ourselves possibly around 10 million years ago; if we found evidence that gorillas shake hands, it would suggest that the handshake dates back to at least the last common ancestor we share with them. This isn't something we've observed them doing, but that doesn't mean they don't do it, just that primatologists haven't managed to catch them at it (or at least haven't written extensively about doing so). The kind of observational work required to study gestures in primates, especially in the wild, is incredibly difficult, and simply habituating the population of primates under study to the presence of humans can take years. For this kind of evolutionary detective work, it's as well to remember that absence of evidence is not evidence of absence.

Ape hands, hugs and kisses

The animal kingdom is littered with examples of hands or appendages being used for practical purposes as well as communication: from the cute memes of otters holding hands to bond (or if you believe the sceptics, aka scientists, for support or thermoregulation) to elephants who utilise their trunks to communicate with each other.[6] But when it comes to bonding and communication, it does not surprise me that primate hands feature so prominently. Primate hands are dexterous, highly functional and important; they are used for locomotion, yes, but also for manipulation and even tool use. Unlike other animals, we primates almost always eat using our hands and often drink with our hands too, and exhibit a number of more specific hand-based behaviours: the slow loris, for example, produces venom under its armpit and uses its hands to rub it all over its body and teeth.[7] Hands are also used in 'handclasp grooming' amongst some chimp and bonobo populations, in which two individuals face each other and raise one arm above their head, clasping the hand of the other for an extended period as they groom.[8]

From hugging to begging (hand stretched, palm upwards), there are a number of gestures we share with chimps. We know that bonobos, chimpanzees, gorillas and orangutans all use their hands to communicate, even if we are only starting to understand what their gestures and signs mean. Great-ape greeting behaviour, too, is centred around close and intimate touch, and appears deeply familiar to us. Depending on how close chimps are, it isn't unusual for contact to be initiated by touching hands or for hugs to be used as a greeting: a matriarch chimp would offer her hand to the primatologist Frans de Waal upon seeing him.[9]

Amongst our other close relatives, the bonobos, famous for their friendly, sex-positive, 1960s hippy vibe, females greet by hugging and rubbing clitorises, a greeting I'm less familiar with in our own species.

From an evolutionary perspective, studying the other great apes allows us to go back in time: the importance that they place not just on hands but also on touch, specifically in greeting behaviour, suggests these are things that have been important to our part of the family tree for millions of years. Perhaps one way of viewing the handshake is simply as a basic unit of touch: a practical, functional and expressive way to channel this deep-seated urge.

We have addressed the 'when', but what about the 'why'? There are plenty of theories as to how we've evolved greeting behaviours; one suggests they might be infantilisms[10] (imitations of the behaviour of infants, such as the way in which chimp mothers offer a hand to their young as a signal for them to jump on their backs), while another suggests they have their basis in mirroring behaviour (important to humans at the best of times, with people who don't know how to reciprocate often being shunned or seen to have committed a faux pas). There are any number of other theories, and I don't particularly buy any of them; some venture so far into unprovable evolutionary psychology that they end up sounding like *Just So* stories. It seems very clear to me that the handshake has a functional biological purpose; it's not an echo of something else, or an artefact – the function is still very much at play in our interactions today. And so I give you smell and touch. In that order.

Smell

Most of us know that smell is important to animals. From dogs to ants, plenty of animals smell each other upon first contact, behaviour that ranges from the awkwardly graphic – sniffing of each other's rear ends – to the endearingly goofy, such as when a horse folds back its upper lip, revealing a gummy smile. The latter is a flehmen response, and it is seen in many mammals; it's actually them taking a whiff, as it helps pheromones and scents get to Jacobson's organ, located above the roof of the mouth. We know that that heightened olfactory ability can even be used between species: dogs, for example, can be trained to detect diseases on humans,[11] including COVID-19,[12] and can even identify emotions such as fear or happiness through our chemosignals (chemical signals emitted by an animal that transmit information to other animals).[13]

But we *Homo sapiens*, with our Mensas, our international space station, our Guggenheims, our Sinatras and our Steve Jobs, *we* have surely evolved beyond smell. Sure, we're familiar with the idea of sexual chemosignals (what some might call sexual pheromones), and their role in helping us choose a partner.[14] Some of you might be like me, with such an extremely sensitive sense of smell that it becomes a burden; there was a time when around a third of the men I rejected owed the rejection partly to their scent (then again, I'm very outdoorsy – some of that crowd seem to take pride in not washing). But that is the extent of smell use in *Homo sapiens*, right? Smell possibly linked to sexual attraction. We aren't animals, after all. Only we *are* animals.

In one of many studies showing how important (and sensitive) our sense of smell is, researchers placed gauze pads under participants' armpits and had them watch films which evoked strong emotions like happiness or fear.[15] Those pads were then presented to other participants, and upon smelling them the sniffers accurately reflected the emotion of the film. Their micro-expressions, tiny changes in the facial muscles, mirrored the emotions felt by the film-watchers. These are reproducible experiments, meaning that they, or variations of them, have been reproduced more than once by different researchers with similar results: the gold standard in science. What I find particularly mind-blowing is that the sniffers' responses appear to have been unconscious: they were mirroring another person's emotions without even *consciously being aware of it*. Although in one experiment conducted by researchers at the Monell Chemical Senses Center in Philadelphia, when participants were asked to select 'the odour of people when they are happy', the participants picked correctly more often than would be expected by chance.[16]

It's not just sweat, either: researchers have shown that human tears also contain chemosignals. In one bizarre study, they collected 'negative-emotion-related odourless tears' from women (I look forward to a country-music song with this title), and then showed men pictures of women. The men exposed to these negative-emotion-related tears reported that the pictured women's faces had less sex appeal and that they personally were less aroused by them (which was confirmed physiologically, including with MRI scans).[17] I'm personally thrilled to hear that research money was used to scientifically answer the question 'Are crying women sexy?'

We think of human communication as being about language and gesture, but this is really a result of our obsession with human exceptionalism – the idea that humans are categorically different from all the other species with whom we share this planet. It is just narcissism: we haven't evolved our way out of being animals. In a wider evolutionary context, none of these experiments' results are surprising. Chemosignals in non-human animals and in humans are essentially a form of social communication; some researchers have hypothesised that chemosignals are part of a survival strategy: if an individual feels fear or disgust, he or she releases a fear or disgust chemosignal that functions in part to communicate this emotion to the group. In this way, the idea of 'emotional contagion' – when we see euphoria, fear or anger rippling through a large crowd – may well have a chemical basis. This is still very much a functional part of our communication repertoire, even if we mainly experience it subconsciously; it isn't smell on one side and bigger brains, speech and iPhones on the other.

So the reason why we evolved to use our hands for greeting in the form of a handshake, rather than, say, celebratory jazz hands, may well be that handshakes (as well as hugs and kisses) have a practical biological purpose related to smell. It seems very likely that the *touch* involved in the handshake acts as a delivery system, a vector, for those chemosignals. Researchers at the Weizmann Institute in Israel were able to show that handshakes are enough to transfer body odour from one person to another. They also covertly filmed 271 participants greeting each other; each was placed in a room and greeted with or without a handshake, and then observed while they were left in the room on their own. Participants were more likely to smell their hands after shaking hands than when they greeted without touching. It didn't appear to be a conscious action, and manifested in actions like touching their noses more after shaking hands, compared with those who were greeted without a handshake. To further test this, the researchers measured nasal airflow, and found that face-touching resulted in people breathing in twice as much air through their nostrils – so face-touching wasn't just a nervous reaction, what some researchers have called 'a form of displacement stress response'.[18]

Touch

Beyond the practical transfer of chemosignals, touch is, of course, enormously important to us in its own right; during the COVID-19 pandemic the idea of 'skin hunger' – where you are touched less than you need, creating a craving for more physical human contact – rose to prominence. For the first few months of lockdown, most of my friends who sheepishly confessed to breaking social-distancing restrictions in London were doing it because they needed comforting. In those months of the pandemic I could count on two hands the number of times I'd touched another human being. The first hug of lockdown I received came after my aunt passed away; the first hug I offered was to someone going through a break-up. Videos of grandchildren inventing COVID-safe contraptions to hug grandparents went viral, illustrating something that most of us felt: that the lack of touch was not just sad, but viscerally painful.

So, touch matters; we might all vary in the extent to which we enjoy being touched – and whom we can tolerate being touched by – but it is undoubtedly something that is important for our mental health and even for child development. But what of the physiology and biochemistry of touch?

Tiffany Field, the founder of the Touch Research Institute at the University of Miami, explains that movement on the skin triggers the vagus nerve, which is connected to every major organ. A handshake or hug 'slows down the heart. It goes to the GI [gastrointestinal] tract and helps digestion. It helps our emotional expressions – our facial expressions and our vocal expressions. It enhances serotonin, the natural antidepressant in our system.'[19] Vagus-nerve activity is also linked to reducing cortisol, the primary stress hormone, and we all know the field day that stress has on our health.

Other studies have shown that oxytocin, a hormone linked to social bonding, trust and protective instincts, is released as a result of touch. In turn, this releases dopamine (a hormone and neurotransmitter originally thought to be linked to pleasure, but now understood to be more about regulating motivation). The media sometimes refer to oxytocin as the love, cuddle or trust hormone,[20] but it's important to note that it is more complicated than that: it is also linked to increased suspicion of people seen as outsiders. Dutch participants in a study who received a dose of it via a nasal spray were more positive about fictional Dutch characters and more negative about Arab- or German-named characters;[21] basically, oxytocin is your cuddly, racist grandparent. Technically it might be more accurate to describe oxytocin as a social-bonding hormone rather than a 'love hormone' – with the understanding that it can have positive and negative effects. So, in layman's terms, we can probably say that touch leads to the release of hormones associated with social bonding ... and you'll get a bit of a warm, fuzzy high off it.

The association between oxytocin, bonding and increased affection for a trusted group of 'insiders' is particularly interesting when you think of the role of the handshake in its more modern contexts. As a field of study, touch is compelling because it is not confined to biochemistry or psychology but extends to subjects like management and business as well, resulting in some rather interesting experiments. Paul Zak, Professor of Economic Psychology and Management in the Center for Neuroeconomics Studies at Claremont Graduate University in Claremont, California, spent $6,000 on massages in order to see whether they affected people's behaviour in a pay-it-forward type of trust experiment. (He points out that, as the architect of the experiment, he never received a massage.) Participants could choose to either keep for themselves a sum of money given to them in an online account, or transfer it over to a perfect stranger; by doing this they would triple it. The stranger could in turn choose to return some of the money to the original participant or keep it all. Those who received a massage returned 243 per cent more money to the person who trusted them; the physical contact apparently made them more likely to sacrifice their own interests and share. The massage didn't appear to release oxytocin by itself, but 'primed the brain to release this neurochemical after one received a signal of trust' such as massage or a handshake: together, touch and trust were 'like putting the human oxytocin system on steroids', helping us kick-start – and then sustain – the kind of co-operation which is so vital to our survival and success.[22] There are also experiments that look at touch, business and hospitality, including a number of experiments which show how touch can increase tips. One study showed that a waiter's tips went from an average of 11.5 per cent of the bill without him touching the clientele to just under 15 per cent.[23]

Touch creates comfort, connection and empathy, and its effects are physiological, biochemical and psychological. This also helps us understand why touching – a handshake or hug or 'kiss and make up' after a fight – is so important as a way to resolve conflict. Really, there's not that much difference between two chimps shaking fingers to reconcile after a fight and two world leaders shaking hands over a peace treaty.

But is all touch created equal? Why did we evolve specifically to shake hands, rather than bump fists or elbows (which, as we'll see in Chapter 7, do have some advantages from the evolutionary point of view)? Surely touch, is touch, is touch? Well, not quite. We have more receptors in our fingers, palms and lips than in most of our other body parts, and they are over-represented in the parts of our brain that handle the information we receive from touch. I've shown how touch is a form of information exchange between humans, as well as a way of sparking off rewarding hormonal changes; when we touch each other with the more sensitive parts of our bodies, we gain more value from the interaction. Which is probably why we shake hands and why we weren't elbow-bumping in the Palaeolithic. This also helps us understand the hierarchy of touch – why the handshake is more formal and distanced than the hug, which encompasses so much more surface area and carries more emotional significance. If touch was a currency, the hug and kiss are riding high … and the elbow bump is the pound sterling after the Brexit vote (which left me looking at my bank balance while abroad in the USA aghast and wondering if I had been robbed). We primates yearn for touch, and the elbow bump really is the poor man's handshake.

Gesture and body language

I want to force the reader into a paradigm shift in how we see the handshake. So I'm only now writing about the handshake as a *gesture*, because for too long we've seen it as little else. We have been reductionist in our approach: not taking into account the multiple biological reasons why we shake hands. But even in its history as a gesture, there is more to the handshake than meets the eye.

Gesturing, moving our bodies in a way that conveys an idea or feeling, is a part of our communication repertoire. It is linked to verbal language: functional MRI scanning has shown that symbolic gestures and spoken language are processed by a common neural system. There is also something quite peculiar about some gestures, in that they can appear in human behaviour without being learnt – in a way that, say, language can't. The ethologist Irenäus Eibl-Eibesfeldt observed Sabine, a congenitally deaf and blind girl, stretching her hand and pushing it back, palms facing outwards, in a gesture of rejection – a gesture she had never seen, but just knew.[24] For a highly social species like ours, it might be advantageous to have a few truly instinctive gestures that are universally understood regardless of differences in language. As our species formed larger and larger social groups and travelled further and further across our planet, meeting new groups of people – people they weren't related to and didn't necessarily know – along the way, handshakes, like a few other gestures, may well have proved to be highly translatable shorthand. Presumably there are times when a gesture is also just quicker at conveying a positive meaning than spoken words.

The Harvard psychologist Professor Steven Pinker gives

another perspective, pointing to Darwin's principle of 'antithesis': the idea that, for example, 'in order to display a friendly, non-threatening intent, animals often evolve a display that is the joint-for-joint, muscle-for-muscle opposite of their display for aggression'. These displays are involuntary. Cats, for instance, stand upright arching their backs and rub against your leg when they are being friendly, with their tails erect, whereas when they attack they do the opposite – they crouch, ready to pounce, with a horizontal tail. Darwin argued that shrugging was an example: when you know something and are feeling sure of yourself and assertive, your shoulders tend to stand tall and back. Now consider the handshake: your hand is open – the opposite of a fist – and you are physically close to the other person, not sizing them up from a safe distance. Pinker adds:

> Displays guided by Darwinian antithesis are just those that spread germs – contact, proximity, and exposure of the mouth and nose – whereas sanitary conventions like fist-bumps and elbow-taps go against the grain of intuitive friendliness. That explains why, at least in my experience, people accompany these gestures with a little laugh, as if to reassure each other that the superficially aggressive displays are new conventions in a contagious time and offered in a spirit of camaraderie.[25]

Certainly, the fist bump and the handshake 'look' like opposite displays.

Psychology

Just like our travelling ancestors, we still live in a world where we constantly meet new people, people we don't yet know very much about. And, just as they did, we still need to hazard a guess as to their intentions, character and trustworthiness. Just as often, we want *them* to like *us*. Body language – as well as gesture – can play an important part, but the science also shows that there is something uniquely psychologically comforting about the handshake.

The positive benefits of the handshake cut both ways. The researchers Florin and Sanda Dolcos at the Neuroscience Lab at the University of Illinois studied those observing (as opposed to those participating in) a handshake; this removed factors like smell and touch, meaning they could focus on the psychological impact only. They found that starting a social interaction with a handshake not only makes a 'favorable interaction' more likely, 'it also diminishes the impact of a negative impression. Many of our social interactions may go wrong for a reason or another, and a simple handshake preceding them can give us a boost' and mitigate 'the negative impact of possible misunderstandings'. By tracking activity in the nucleus accumbens, a reward-processing region of the brain, the researchers saw greater activity in the region when a handshake occurred.[26]

Handshakes are so effective in building trust that one study showed that you could even substitute one of the parties for a robot – *an inanimate object* – and still increase the trust in mock house sales. One important thing to note here is that touch was still involved: the robot's hand vibrated during a handshake, creating a connection between the two individuals which increased co-operation and trustworthiness. (In other words, they were less likely to screw each other over.)

A handshake as old as time

So, let's recap. The handshake used by our last common ancestor with chimps 7 million years ago may not be the exact handshake – with its choreography of grasp and pump – that we see today. Perhaps it was a handshake *sans* the pump, more 'hand' than 'shake'; but even this proto-hand-shake would be recognisable to us. Given that the handshake is used across many cultures, both human (contacted and uncontacted) and non-human, it is high time we stopped seeing it as a learnt cultural tradition and instead as some-thing deeply biological in origin, perhaps even imprinted in our DNA in the same way that language use is. Draw-ing on evidence from multiple scientific fields, it's clear the handshake has many biological purposes, from a chemosig-nal delivery system to a quick shorthand between strangers to stimulating the reward centres of our brains (even when we're apparently selling our house to a robot). Perhaps this is one of the reasons why the handshake has such longevity, presence and prominence in our own species: it is a one-stop shop, a basic unit of touch. It lacks the full impact of two other units of touch, the kiss and the embrace – when we are most physically connected, covering most surface area, with our noses closest together – but the handshake is quicker and safer to execute, more versatile, and wider in its poten-tial application.

However, you may be asking yourself: if the handshake is biological, if it is so important, so old and so vital for communication, social bonding and so on, why don't cultures in the Far East traditionally engage in it? That is an incredibly important question. We can have a genetic proclivity for a certain behaviour as a result of evolutionary programming, but then culturally we stop that behaviour, as in turn do our children (while simultaneously inheriting the genes that programme for the opposite). Biologically, for example, we are meat eaters, with canine teeth that help us shear and tear it. But we know that large populations in India have historically been vegetarians, that many ancient religions contain prohibitions about particular kinds of meat, and that today there is a growing population of vegans who use their canines only for tearing into tofu burgers. The handshake's demise amongst populations in the Far East could be the result of just this kind of cultural evolution.

The first thing to note is that, in many parts of the Far East, not just handshakes but all physical contact in greetings between strangers is traditionally shunned, something which is assumed to be a form of respect. If we say touch is important in greetings, and handshakes are units of touch, traditionally countries like Japan and Thailand appear to employ no units whatsoever. Over the early weeks of the pandemic in 2020, I would often find myself in conversations about handshakes with other scientists, a few of whom (including the ecologist Dr Kay Van Damme) had independently come up with an interesting theory. Perhaps the touch-avoidant cultures of the Far East didn't evolve out of respect at all: perhaps it was a cultural response to similar ancient epidemic events, which created a temporary behavioural change that then stuck. Touch became taboo, but after a few generations nobody remembers the reason why. A similar theory suggests that the Jewish taboo against eating shellfish – a very useful and nutritious food source for those with access to it, used by earlier species of human as well as our prehistoric ancestors – was originally a response to food poisoning.

To explore this further, I reached out to a friend who is a Tibetan anthropologist. He clarified that Tibetans sometimes hold hands amongst friends, but generally keep hugging to a minimum; he could, however, think of one exception. His father was a Tibetan refugee when he finally saw his beloved brother after decades apart; '*then* they hugged'. He touched on something fascinating: Tibetans have long been aware of the concept of *treep*, which can very roughly be translated as 'germs'; and so not only did they avoid wearing the clothes of people who were ill, but they traditionally often carried their own bowls and utensils on their person, in some regions wearing their spoon around their neck. Whether in your home or the home of another, those are the utensils that you (and only you) used. Historically, Tibetans were impressive in their understanding of science, physiology and the human body, and well ahead of the Western world in this regard; their understanding of anatomy was partly informed by the practice of sky burial, which involved dismembering the dead and leaving them for vultures to consume. Of course, their ownership of personal utensils and crockery could also have been due to their semi-nomadic lifestyle and low population density, meaning that they needed to carry those items with them, and the concept of *treep* might have appeared for different reasons. I can't help but wonder. Because you might indeed expect a population highly literate in human physiology and who – as humans have throughout history – faced a particularly significant epidemic event or events to respond with just these kinds of behavioural changes.

If the less-touch-based greeting cultures of the Far East do reflect divergent evolution as a response to a previous epidemic, we can't be sure of the other conditions in which that massive cultural shift occurred. Was it due to small population size, and the result of some kind of bottleneck or founding event? Or could it have been a political incentive, say in the form of a directive given by a powerful ruler (think of the speed with which the Nazi salute was adopted in Germany)? Presumably this kind of behavioural change takes a long time, so if we can trace it back to a contagion of some kind, it must have been either a really long, protracted epidemic over many, many years or many epidemics over a number of years.

The theory presented in this chapter – that the handshake is deeply imprinted in our DNA, is biological and not just cultural, and at least 7 million years old – draws on multiple scientific disciplines. And the result, to my mind, is clear: there needs to be a paradigm shift in the way we see handshakes. Popular literature is obsessed with the handshake as a symbol of trust and as evidence of not carrying weaponry. The handshake's symbolism is significant, as we shall see in the next chapter; but 'takes' that don't mention the important role of biology and evolution or that consider Western missionaries to be the founding fathers of the handshake are lazy, badly researched and oft-recycled garbage. The handshake's origin story is in much deeper time.

2

Symbolism: What Does the Handshake Mean?

So, the handshake has a biological purpose – and very probably a biological origin too. But that doesn't mean the handshake doesn't have a symbolic meaning, value or purpose; it's just that symbolism is only a part of the handshake's story. After all, we eat because it's a biological imperative, but my friends still remember one birthday when I bought myself a wedding cake. They thought I was making a feminist statement, but it was an accident. I really like profiteroles and didn't realise, until it arrived, that what I had bought was a three-foot-high tower of them ... so a wedding cake! Birthday cakes, accidental wedding cakes ... they go beyond nutrition. Similarly, the handshake carries associations for us that go beyond the biological – to the diplomatic, artistic and (yes) even the marital. We are well aware and conscious of these symbolic meanings, unlike the handshake's biological purposes of, say, being a vector for chemosignals or triggering touch receptors. A symbolic gesture requires us to recognise a shared and accepted meaning: agreement, acceptance, submission. The meanings attached to the handshake have varied over time, sometimes in ways that seem surprising to us today. But one thing is a constant – they are always good: there's never been any room for anything other than positivity in the handshake.

Deconstructing the handshake

It's impossible to discuss the symbolism of the handshake without first talking about the symbolism of the human hand. The human hand has, of course, been on an evolutionary journey, which for some animals resulted in wings or flippers, and for us (and some of our closer relatives, like chimps) culminated in a palm, four dexterous fingers and our famously opposable thumb. The primate hand is fascinating in its own right, having evolved an opposable thumb for grasping branches and swapping its claws for nails. But *our* hands went further: as we became bipedal, and they began to be freed up from the responsibility of locomotion, the human thumb, specifically, lengthened relative to the other fingers and was able to touch them. This revolutionised what we could do with our hands: we now had unrivalled grasp and dexterity, and with it an ability to manipulate not just our hands but the world around us. The philosopher Emmanuel Kant described our hands as 'man's outer brain',[1] and indeed, the earliest species in our genus *Homo* is called *Homo habilis*; as *Homo* means 'man' and *habilis* means 'handy', this was literally the world's first *handy man*. While our genus is not the only one to practise tool use, only humans have used their hands to create increasingly complex technology. We often marvel at the wing, and, to be fair, it's not a bad effort. But I'm telling you, if birds had our mental abilities, they would be filled with awe and wonder at the human hand and what it has created. From the Iron Age to the iPhone, the world we have created around us is truly an ode to these unique appendages.

We use our hands not only to shape the world around us, but also to describe it: old texts might refer to hand-spans as a unit of measurement, and the word 'digit' comes from the Latin word *digitus* meaning finger or toe.[2] Beyond this, the hand can help us express or emphasise the words we speak more effectively. I'm Arab, and therefore basically came out of the womb very sociable, covered in hummus and gesticulating wildly. At times when TV presenting, my hand movements can be very distracting so I sit on them. But hand gestures are an integral part of body language and not being able to use them feels unnatural and even frustrating, as if you aren't communicating with everything at your disposal. And there are plenty of hand gestures that have a clear meaning in their own right: a thumbs up, flipping the bird, a hand up in class and, of course, the handshake.

Is it any wonder, then, that our hands have such profound meaning: that we lay a hand on a holy book to take an oath in court (and then raise it while speaking under oath), that we used to ask for someone's hand in marriage, that some of my more optimistic friends put their faith in palmistry and that, in many cultures, an image of the hand wards off the evil eye. The Mindanao tribes of the Philippines returned with their enemies' hands after fighting, while the Itneg (Tinguian) also of the Philippines would make liquor with the parts of the body thought to represent strength: the brain, ear lobes and finger joints.[3] Given all this, it seems less serendipitous and more like poetry that something on our hands – our fingerprints – are the best unique identifiers going. Even identical twins, indistinguishable at the DNA level, will still have different fingerprints.

The art of the hand(shake)

In the previous chapter I said that handshakes haven't been preserved in the fossil and archaeological records. That's true. But what we do have, time and time (and time) again, in different cultures, thousands of years apart, is an obsession with hands in rock and cave art. Handprints and hand stencils, often in red ochre, litter walls from Australia to the Americas; sometimes tens of thousands of years old, they literally span space and time. And even species: Maltravieso Cave in Spain contains seventy-one hand stencils, one of which dates to at least 66,000 years ago, making it the oldest cave painting in the world. But *Homo sapiens* weren't living in Spain 66,000 years ago: Neanderthals were. The earliest cave and rock art involved geometric shapes, stick-figure humans and animals as well as hands, but even when the early artistic repertoire matures, the hands remain. People often don't realise that much famous prehistoric art, such as the spotted horses in Pech Merle, is actually surrounded by handprints.

I've seen the work of these Palaeolithic Banksies – and their hand obsession – replicated all over the world. In late 2019, I visited two rock-art sites in Serranía de La Lindosa in Colombia, one called Cerro Azul, the other so newly discovered that it had no name. The archaeologist Professor José Iriarte was predicting that the latter might be the largest cache of rock art in South America, and I was one of the very first outsiders to see it. Lo and behold, amongst all the drawings and abstract art, there in red ochre were many, many handprints.

As I stood there and held my own hand up, just off the wall (so as not to damage the red ochre), I knew that someone had once stood in just this place: perhaps an artist, perhaps a shaman ... perhaps a juvenile delinquent. The handprints are not an interpretation or imaginative work: they are an accurate depiction of a thing that really existed, the most accurate depiction in any cave or rock art. As you stand there, it is as if you are shaking hands with someone who lived thousands of years ago.

The handprints may have had more than one meaning: the mysterious presence of handprints by adults and children as young as two very high up on walls led the researcher Paul Pettitt and his colleagues to conclude that they might have been a way to communicate in dark cave conditions, perhaps giving practical advice and warnings about cave features. (Well! Cliff! Bear!!) Ultimately, we will probably never know exactly what they meant to the people who created them. But what we do know for sure is that there was a fascination with hand motifs; in some locations these motifs come together as overlapping hands, almost as if ascending to heaven. At others, as seen in Cerro Azul, there appears to be a row of people holding hands (a very male row, as made abundantly clear by some generous artistic licence).[4]

The iconography of the hand is still clearly associated with numerous spiritual and religious traditions today, from the multiple arms with which Hindu deities are often depicted to the body language of worship itself. This seems to echo the expressive potential of our hands: in Christian prayer they are placed together and pointed up, while in Muslim prayer they are out, palms facing up and slightly cupped, as if begging. In *The Creation of Adam*, Michelangelo's famous Sistine Chapel fresco, God and Adam are almost touching hands; the connection, breaching all that distance, is generally thought to represent the spark of life being transmitted to humankind. But the critic Ed Simon provides my favourite interpretation: 'It's fun to imagine Michelangelo's Sistine Chapel painting of God and Adam as a depiction of the last few seconds before history's first handshake.'[5]

Myths, legends and … handshakes

A common origin story for the handshake pinpoints its beginnings in medieval times, as a way of demonstrating you didn't have a weapon. Your right hand is your sword hand, so you opened your palm to show nothing was inside it and then you shook it up and down to dislodge any weapons hidden up your sleeve. According to this 'weapons theory' of greetings, tipping the hat comes from raising the visor of your helmet – showing that you weren't 'war-ready' – while the wave is about showing, from a distance, that you weren't brandishing a weapon. The story appears to have been in circulation since at least the late nineteenth century; *Rochester Post-Express*, back in 1887, stated: 'In early and barbarous times, when every savage or semi-savage was his own lawgiver, judge, soldier and policeman … [people would offer] the hand that wields the sword, the dagger, the club, tomahawk or other weapons of war. Each did this to show that the hand was empty, and that neither war nor treachery was intended.'[6] Sadly, while a rather convenient explanation, upon examination this notion is basically nonsense.

Symbolism: What Does the Handshake Mean?

For a start, as we have seen, the handshake predates not only the Bronze and Iron Ages, but the Stone Age as well – so it was around well before the kind of weaponry we are talking about. But even were that not the case, there are obvious practical and logical problems with the theory. The need to prove that there are no weapons in your hand suggests that the other person is viewed as a threat; but the handshake itself results in you getting up close and personal, offering both of you the opportunity and means to attack (as we will see in Chapter 6, where I deal with the tragic case of President McKinley). Your right hand might be empty initially, but what is to stop it from reaching for your sword or a dagger as soon as you're within range? Indeed, your right hand might even be held in someone else's, but if your left is free what's to stop it from reaching for the weapon on your person? Not to mention the damage that can be done with a pair of bare hands! The argument is fundamentally flawed, unless one accepts that the handshake is basically a gentlemanly game of chicken. Taking a more anthropological perspective, there's plenty of evidence of cultures that do use weapons or 'aggression' in greetings: the traditional Maori greeting involves raising a weapon, for example.

It's unclear to me how this origin story ever got traction, but then I guess not everyone has watched both their brothers turn up to their Birmingham schools on Comic Relief Day wearing a traditional Yemeni outfit complete with an elaborate dagger on their belts. My younger brother did this for three years running, winning 'best outfit' every year, naturally. Only one year did his teacher take the dagger off him and pass it to the head teacher's office until the end of the day 'for safe keeping'. There was an enviably laid-back approach to safety in Brummie schools during the 1990s – I guess they weren't expecting parents to supply the weapons. However, there's one indisputable reason why the handshake's origins aren't found in the knightly traditions of the medieval period: the historical record clearly shows that, in fact, we've been at it for millennia.

Mesopotamia

The earliest known depiction of an unmistakable, unambiguous handshake harks back to two ancient Mesopotamian powers: the Babylonian and Assyrian Empires. A sculptured relief from the ninth century BC, found at Nimrud in northern Iraq, and now housed at the Iraqi Museum in Baghdad, depicts a handshake between the Assyrian King Shalmaneser III and the Babylonian King Marduk-Zakir-Shumi I.

Carved into the dais that supported the throne at Fort Shalmaneser, the relief commemorates a victory: Shalmaneser had helped his ally Marduk-Zakir-Shumi quell a rebellion by his brother, Marduk-Bel-Usati. Behind each king the relief depicts a sort of guard of honour (presumably) comprising courtiers, advisors or guards, some of whom are carrying weapons. Its prominent positioning in the throne room shows it was clearly of importance to Shalmaneser III, and the inscription suggests that this victory was his alone, as if he single-handedly returned Marduk-Zakir-Shumi's throne to him. Historians have argued that it was Shalmaneser's most prestigious moment, even if he was overstating his role just a touch: the peak of his political career, a point of pride, an international relations coup and a military victory. To our twenty-first-century eyes, the scene on the relief is completely familiar – this was a handshake of state, whose immortalisation in stone and placement on the throne suggest that diplomatic handshakes have a deep history. It might as well have taken place in the White House Rose Garden, being broadcast on NBC or the BBC instead of carved into stone.

Given that Marduk-Zakir-Shumi was a lesser, foreign king, the head of what was probably a client state, the portrayal here of two men shaking hands as equals has confused some archaeologists. They have argued that it can't be Marduk-Zakir-Shumi, because he would more likely be kneeling or kissing in homage.[7] But in his *Nimrud 1962* monograph, the archaeologist David Oates points out that, at the time, the handshake did not necessarily symbolise equality: '"To strike the hand of another" signified, in Near Eastern diplomacy of the second millennium BC, the formal rejection of a proferred alliance or the rupture of an existing relationship.' Thus, it's possible to infer that 'the clasping of hands was employed to confirm an international agreement even when the two parties were not equals'.[8] And so the first record of a diplomatic handshake isn't about parity, but carries a different meaning, albeit one we would recognise: 'sealing the deal'. And its portrayal for all to see, decorating the literal seat of power in Shalmaneser's kingdom, was another familiar iteration of the handshake: it's essentially a propaganda exercise.[9]

Greece

The oldest textual references to handshakes are found in ancient Greece, in Homer's *Iliad* and *Odyssey*, usually dated to around the eighth century BC, where they symbolise trust, comfort and pledging allegiance. The best-known example comes from the *Iliad*, when the Trojan Glaucus and the Greek hero Diomedes meet on the battlefield: initially set for single combat, when they discover that Diomedes' grandfather hosted Glaucus's own ancestor, the hostility dissolves in 'friendly words'; 'they sprang from their chariots, grasped one another's hands, and plighted friendship'.[10] According to one scholar, the handshake 'if nothing else, has made the meeting of Glaucus and Diomedes famous … [with] its unique emphasis on mutual understanding, the scene is widely regarded as an oasis of common decency amid the war-ethos of the surrounding books'.[11]

However, it's not until around the fifth century BC that these references were followed by an explosion in handshake iconography. Referred to as *dexiosis*, 'to take the right hand', the ancient Greek handshake is portrayed as occurring between the living and the dead, between mortals and gods, close relatives, strangers and men and women. The Classical archaeologist Janet Burnett Grossman defines it as a 'gesture symbolizing connectedness'.[12] As well as the multiple meanings of the handshake that we would all recognise today (friendship, solidarity, alliance and peace between enemies), there are two which are less familiar to us: in funerary art and to symbolise marriage. 'You may now shake the hand of the bride' isn't something we are accustomed to. Indeed, if handshakes signified marriage, most of us would suddenly find ourselves entertaining polygamy. In both cases, *dexiosis* seems related to the idea of lasting union or relationship; in funerary art and on gravestones, the handshake was often depicted taking place between a living person and a departed family member. While its significance is not entirely obvious, it perhaps symbolised a farewell, or an ongoing connection – a reminder of a bond, a meeting in the afterlife?

It's clear that by the Classical period, the handshake already had multiple meanings – its flexibility and versatility as a symbol may well have been deliberately exploited by artists to create a sense of ambiguity.[13] This diversity in the symbolic meaning of handshakes – although always all positive – doesn't appear to be a modern or even a human innovation: when undertaking research into primate handshaking, Dr Cat Hobaiter also found that amongst chimps it has positive but adaptable meanings that are hard to define as a result. What is likely instead is that this generally positive ambiguity may be one of the handshake's strengths as a symbolic gesture, allowing it to alter somewhat in time and space, keeping a flexibility in meaning that allows it to speak for beings as diverse as a chimp, an ancient Greek warrior and a modern human.

I find myself especially endeared to one particular ancient Greek handshake: a sixth-century BC representation of Herakles shaking hands with Pholos, a centaur who protected the hero against the other centaurs. The amphora which depicts this scene also shows the god of mediators, Hermes, to the right, sitting down as if exhausted by the effort of bringing about the friendly encounter.[14] The proud presence of the mediator is, again, a familiar scene from modern diplomacy – and I suspect this is how Bill Clinton *actually* felt after getting the Palestinians and Israelis to shake hands.

Etruscan and Roman times

Between the fourth and first centuries BC the handshake appears extensively in Etruscan funerary art, in various forms and on various materials; some are ready-made mass-market items, but it appears on tombs and sarcophagi too. The handshake here gives a real insight into the cosmology, or world view, of the time: as a motif, it expresses 'a characteristically Etruscan view of the afterlife'[15] in which children, servants and married couples share space with winged figures, demons and Charun, a spirit of the underworld. The details are fascinating, sometimes even amusing; as the Classicist Glenys Davies puts it, 'Quite often the couple shaking hands are in the presence of both underworld and human figures: the demons may simply stand patiently beside the couple, but sometimes one of them appears to indicate with an impatient gesture that one of the couple is to be taken away.' In yet another example 'thought to commemorate someone who had held magisterial office, the deceased is shown shaking hands with the leader of a procession of officials accompanied by lictors and musicians who, it seems, have all turned out to give him a good send-off'.[16]

In the Roman Empire which followed the Etruscan civilisation, we again see the handshake, now known as *dextrarum iunctio*, in funerary contexts but also in paintings, on coins and in mosaics: in two paintings depicting the rescue of Andromeda from the sea monster Cetus, her father Cepheus shakes the hand of the hero Perseus, perhaps in a manly gesture of gratitude for saving the princess.[17] This is the handshake as a gesture of approval, endorsement, a cousin not far removed of Paul Hollywood's prized

'Hollywood handshake', used by the *Great British Bake Off* star to commend an especially delectable bake.

Handshakes and hierarchy

You may be thinking that the trouble with an image of a handshake is that you can't tell what exactly is going on: is it simply a clasping of hands, or does it include the canonical shake-up-and-down as well? After all, it's not until well into the medieval period in the British Isles that we start to see references to the shaking; it is mentioned in 1513 in the *Dictionary of the Older Scottish Tongue*: 'to schake handis'.[18] As a result, some have raised the question of whether a handclasp is even the same as a handshake – and to them I say: yes it is.[19] Please let's move on.

One of the problems facing the historian of the handshake is that it's hard to tell whether the absence of hand-shaking in the historical record is because it really was absent, or because it was such a banal part of human interaction that it would be akin to saying 'holds the door open' or 'kept eyes open during conversation'. But another reason why things end up missing from the history books has to do with class and status. History is rarely written by the poor and the powerless, and if the 'lower' classes shook hands but the 'upper' classes preferred greetings that reinforced status, hierarchy and pomp, then we might easily get the impression that salutation was all about bows and curtseys.

Which brings me to one of the cheekiest handshakes of all time, and a perfect example of the radical potential of this simple gesture: as a symbolic assertion of equality and a disruptor of hierarchy. *The Anonimalle Chronicle*, an anonymous history written in Anglo-French, describes a scene in York in 1381, during the Great Revolt led by Wat Tyler against Richard II. In it, Tyler approaches Richard, takes his hand vigorously and shakes it. At the same time he calls the monarch 'brother'.[20] It would be like calling the Queen 'love' or 'comrade', but about a thousand times more shocking in an age of divine right, when the king was an absolute monarch and deemed to be the direct representative of God on earth.

There is a clear and interesting interplay between society, hierarchy and the handshake or, more specifically, hierarchical societies and the handshake. Medieval Europe was for most of its existence a feudal society with a deep-rooted social order which manifested in greeting behaviour: kneeling, bowing, curtseying and a gesture which involved placing both hands together, palm to palm, between the palms of another in an act of subservience known as *immixtio manuum*.[21] The symmetry (or asymmetry) of gestures was hugely significant, and helped to establish and reinforce a pecking order; in fact, as one historian puts it, 'symmetrical uses of the body were analogous to a legally valid process of establishing equal status'[22] and were mostly used in diplomatic relations and between rulers – which certainly puts a new slant on Wat's chummy handshake.

The significance of gestural symmetry and hierarchy is something that's still in play today – a mutual bow in the Far East is about reciprocal humility and respect – and not just in the human sphere: according to Frans de Waal, male chimps greet the alpha chimp with lowered heads.[23]

What this shows – whether you're a bolshy 'peasant' at the head of a rebel army or an anxious beta chimp trying to make sure you don't get your face bitten off – is that, whether we recognise it or not, our greeting behaviour is performative: it projects something about our understanding of the world. Nowadays, of course, we live in a vastly more equal society than the Middle Ages, which makes it even odder, to my mind, that we still bow or curtsey to the Queen. It seems particularly strange to me because as a child I was constantly told that Islam strictly forbids prostration to anyone but God (you don't even kneel to prophets), and this was ingrained in me; I remember when I was younger worrying about what I would do if I ever met the Queen. On the other hand my classmates seemed burdened with the question of what they would do if they ever met Boyzone. There are, of course, other dissenters: Cherie Blair was widely reported to have refused to curtsey to the Queen after her husband became prime minister in 1997, as did the Australian Prime Minister Julia Gillard in 2011. But in general we still seem to have an odd blind spot about this practice; when Theresa May curtseyed to Prince William in 2018 the press focused on her awkward, incredibly low execution. But I see your 'awkward stance' and I raise you the fact that it's backward, jarring and, yes, gross that a grown woman who was elected to office by the people of this country as our second female prime minister was asked to prostrate herself before a prince half her age.[24]

A quiet kind of radicalism was developing within the history of the handshake; in societies with deep, inbuilt inequalities there was symbolic power in a symmetrical gesture whereby you cannot help but meet as equals. Quakerism, a Christian religious movement, appeared at a time which felt to some like the end of the world: a civil war between

Charles I and Parliament culminated in the beheading of the monarch. Radical religious ideologies abounded. The initial ideas of the Quakers would not be entirely recognisable to us today – let's say they have mellowed – but one thing has been consistently true of them: their commitment to egalitarianism. It's no surprise that a handshake came to play a significant part in their world view. In *The History of the Rise, Increase, and Progress of the Christian People called Quakers*, William Sewel writes of 'their plainness, and the decency and simplicity of their conversation; they do not use the ceremonies and salutations of the church of England, but shake hands freely, and converse together as brothers and sisters, that are sprung of the same royal seed'.[25]

We can derive a sense of how the handshake was viewed at the time from John Bulwer's 1644 book *Chirologia: Or the Natural Language of the Hand*, which states that 'to shake the given hand is an expression usual in friendship, peaceful love, benevolence, salutation, entertainment and bidding welcome, reconciliation, congratulation, giving thanks, valediction and well-wishing'. These are, as we might expect, all positive connotations, and it makes perfect sense that the Quakers, also known as Friends, would cleave to a gesture like this in their search for a less hierarchical greeting; today, a handshake still marks the end of a Quaker service.

Some have argued that it was the Quakers who popularised the handshake in North America, after they arrived there as Puritan settlers fleeing persecution in England. This is often presented as something of a transatlantic cultural coup, although on closer investigation it seems unlikely. For one thing, the handshake was already widely in existence; but we also need to look at the wider cultural and social context before deciding why it started to replace other gestures. Andy Scott, author of *One Kiss or Two?*, writes: 'it's no accident that the rise of the handshake coincided with the rise of democratic ideals', and I tend to agree; on both sides of the Atlantic there appeared to be growing resistance to 'performing' hierarchical greetings, with dissenters refusing to comply even if in court. Depending on your perspective, this was either a powerful act of egalitarian resistance or insolence and rudeness. The Quakers may occupy centre stage in this narrative because they were conspicuously hostile and contemptuous towards hierarchy, refusing en masse even to take off their hats or use the term 'Your Grace', so it may be that they are simply a better-documented and better-organised example of a wider trend.[26]

This move towards democracy was of course a moment of huge political, cultural and social significance. Thomas Jefferson, one of America's Founding Fathers, who went on to become the third US president, further popularised the handshake, which he favoured over other courtly gestures. In this he diverged, possibly intentionally, from George Washington, who didn't like shaking hands and 'preferred to bow from the waist; this habit caused his critics to suspect monarchical tendencies in the first president'.[27] Jefferson was the principal author of the 1776 Declaration of Independence, including the line 'all men are created equal'; he was deeply committed to egalitarianism (at least, for the white inhabitants of the country) and anti-aristocratic. By the time of the French Revolution in 1789, during which the approving Jefferson was American Minister to France,[28] the image of clasped hands had come to stand for one of the key revolutionary values: *fraternité*, or brotherhood.[29]

The handshake played a role in other egalitarian struggles, too; it is interesting to note how, after the rise of the suffragette movement and campaign for female emancipation, we see the de-popularisation, and eventual extinction, of older, more gendered greeting behaviours. Historically, in the UK and USA the handshake seems to have been more common as a greeting between men;[30] of course, greetings amongst women are under-represented in the historical record. Women and men of equal social status greeted each other in any number of ways – curtseys and bows, a kiss on the hand or tip of the hat. It's important to note that there is little symmetry in these gestures, and they are clearly intended to underline fundamental differences between the genders even when they ostensibly appear to be a sign of submission to the female participant.[31] In fact, there seems to have been a semi-explicit understanding that delicate women were simply not up to the rigours of a handshake. In 1870, *Harper's Weekly* cautions women against spirited hand-shaking: 'It is for them to receive homage, not to give it.' As the arc of history has slowly turned towards equality, the handshake – simple, versatile, positive, gender-neutral and egalitarian – has been a clear beneficiary.

You'll note that in this section I have chiefly dealt with European and anglophone history. This is not to suggest that the history of the handshake is a Western one; indeed, in the Muslim world in the early modern period hugs and handshakes were very much practised, and blasphemous bows were frowned upon. But the development of the handshake as an egalitarian symbol is a Western story.

The handshake's modern symbolism and purpose

Out of these deep and diverse roots has grown the handshake as we know it today: the gesture that can be everything from a 'hi' to a 'goodbye', the crescendo of a peace treaty, a way of offering condolences or respect, of saying 'I see you', the safe-for-work version of 'kiss and make up'. It not only tells us something about each other's intentions but helps us structure our interactions, forming 'social parentheses'[32] that book-end an encounter or conclude a statement that someone completely and utterly agrees with. It covers business deals, bets, gratitude and sportsmanship, as well as having a profoundly symbolic role in international diplomacy and the struggle for civil rights. Its various meanings and uses, however, are universally positive, and the handshake always suggests civility (which is perhaps why, when the likes of Donald Trump or Narendra Modi attempt to turn it into a display of machismo, the results are so embarrassing). I can't put it better than *Practical Illustrations of Rhetorical Gesture and Action* did in 1807: 'This gesture is rich in signification, for the hand is the tongue of hearty good will.'[33]

This partly explains why the refusal to shake hands with someone – a staple of what the researcher Sheryl N. Hamilton has termed 'Pandemic Culture' – feels so hurtful. As Hamilton puts it: 'the refusal to shake hands … renders the offerer an outsider, a threat to the community, with whom one would be contaminated by touch, and to whom a handshake would have granted legitimacy and access'. This explains why we so often feel we have to explain why we don't want to shake hands, for example when our own hands are dirty or cold.[34] Even when there is a very real danger of contamination, losing the handshake still somehow under-cuts our ability to relate to one another – on a symbolic level, of course, but also on the basic human level where we say, 'I like you enough to touch you.' And this, perhaps, is the reason for the handshake's extreme resilience through-out millennia. Put simply, it's too useful a symbol of positive social interaction to us and we want to do it too much to dispense with it permanently. Nothing can touch it for lon-gevity except the embrace and the kiss – and it beats both of those on sheer versatility. Today, that versatility is perhaps best demonstrated by its critical procedural importance in three professional areas: sport, business and politics.

Sport

As a symbol of civility, the handshake helps us to draw a line under hostility and separate play from reality – two consid-erations which are clearly appropriate in sport. It is pretty standard across most forms of sport for a handshake to draw the game to a close: it is, in fact, seen as a 'ritual of closure' by some academics.[35] This is required because there are undoubtedly similarities between games and conflict: there are different sides; there is often violence or the illusion of it; there are hormones pumping and a certain amount of skill determines the winner. Therefore, to return to everyday life – in which it's generally frowned upon to tackle your opponent to the ground – we use a gesture of civility, co-operation and mutual respect. It wasn't a real fight, it's *just sport*. So you shake hands, and you live to see another day. A willingness to shake hands is one of the key signifiers of good sportsman-ship: a commitment to abide by the rules and respect others.

The business handshake

The business handshake is, like the diplomatic handshake, one of the few kinds of handshake that is its own recognised genre. Within that context, though, the business handshake has several functions, from calling card (if we are to believe a myriad of business books that tell us the handshake is crucial to making a first impression) to sealing the deal.

When we say 'Let's shake on it', after all, we are referring to the depth of the association between the handshake and the deal. Throughout history the handshake has assumed something like legal status, replacing or (more probably) pre-empting the paperwork that would formalise the deal. Relying on a handshake can be a source of pride: the legendary talent agent Irving Paul 'Swifty' Lazar, whose clients included Truman Capote, Madonna and Richard Nixon, once declared, 'I have no contracts with my clients; just a handshake is enough.' To pick another example, it is traditional in parts of Poland for head shepherds to hire helpers and seal the deal with a handshake.[36] Like the 'gentleman's agreement', it is a way of saying 'My word is my bond', a symbol of good faith, respect and trust in the other party. On a more practical level, handshake contracts also made sense in societies in which few people could read or write; widespread literacy is a relatively modern phenomenon.

I would not recommend dispensing with the paperwork myself, having met a few people whose word is, shall we say, not a very robust bond. But, interestingly, the kind of bond of trust represented by the handshake deal is particularly useful if you *are* up to no good, and the handshake in this context is also a sign that something slightly shady is occurring. There are still examples of this amongst some

English share farmers, where informal handshake agreements 'are designed specifically to avoid the attention of the lawyer, the taxman and the agent'.[37] But for all its practical applications, it's probably the handshake's symbolism that earns it its special place in the business world; as Sheryl N. Hamilton sums it up, 'Even at the height of flu season ... the handshake is too essential to the legal performativity undergirding successful business relations to be regulated away.' It seems that 'a businessman's (dirty) hand remains his bond'.[38] So, to some people at least, not to shake is to self-sabotage.

The politician's handshake

Another area in which, it seems, only a handshake will do is politics. This isn't the handshake *between* politicians (Chapters 5 and 6 will give you more on that); this is the 'retail handshake', an extension of retail politics that starts on the campaign trail, and, if all goes well, continues while in office. It is a specific kind of handshake intended to increase and maintain popularity through actual (or, for the cynic, the illusion of) warmth and closeness with the great unwashed. Some politicians have taken it to frankly unbelievable levels: Teddy Roosevelt holds the Guinness World Record for most handshakes by a head of state, as he shook 8,513 hands on the first day of 1907 (though he ruined the illusion somewhat by promptly washing his hands in revulsion).[39] Roosevelt had clearly developed a maximally efficient technique:

> For what must be the three thousandth time, his right arm shoots out. 'Dee-lighted!' Unlike his predecessors,

Symbolism: What Does the Handshake Mean?

Theodore Roosevelt does not limply allow himself to be shaken. He seizes on the fingers of every guest, and wrings them with surprising power. 'It's a very full and very firm grip,' warns one newspaper, 'that might bring a woman to her knees if she wore her rings on her right hand.' The grip is accompanied by a discreet, but irresistible sideways pull, for the President, when he lets go, wishes to have his guest already well out of the way. Yet this lightning moment of contact is enough for him to transmit the full voltage of his charm.

So writes Edmund Morris in *The Rise of Theodore Roosevelt*.[40] He wasn't the only one: the number of handshakes undertaken by Lyndon B. Johnson is said to have left him with swollen, bruised hands at the end of the day.[41] President McKinley's painful-sounding McKinley grip was said to be so efficient that he could shake fifty people's hands in a minute (see p. 110).[42] Whether these enormous numbers are truly plausible (and the cynical scientist in me has her suspicions), the moment of connection created by the retail handshake is so important to the politician that even heads of state are willing to accept the trade-off with their safety to conduct it. President McKinley was, after all, assassinated by someone offering a handshake, and even Donald Trump, a notorious germaphobe who expressed disgust at the idea of the handshake, admitted that 'You can't be a politician and not shake hands'.

In 1958, nearly 3,000 years after the first diplomatic handshake was recorded in stone in ancient Mesopotamia, a French consul was awarded $60,000 in damages for a hand injury 'after proving that handshaking was integral to his career as a diplomat'.[43] Even today, politicians know that they can tweet regularly and be on every TV channel but there is no substitute for the handshake. A political campaign is, after all, an exercise in gaining the public's trust, and the handshake is a way of cultivating that relationship. In turn, people want a 'taste' of their politicians, they want to get a feel for whether they could share a beer with them – and the handshake is the closest you can get to that. We've seen that a handshake might help them do so on a biochemical level, but its chief value here is as a symbol of trust, respect and meeting the general public, at least symbolically, as equals. We might have started shaking hands because of a biological imperative, but we've surely stuck with it because of its power as a symbol. In a democracy, it seems, the handshake still rules.

3

Finger Snaps and Penis Shakes:
Handshakes, Greetings and Cultures

When the COVID-19 pandemic first hit Britain and the USA in February 2020, many columnists seemed delighted to wave goodbye to the handshake. The anthropologist in me was amused – how very Anglo-Saxon. The French kiss, the Italians embrace, the Gulf Arabs touch noses, yet we thought we had it bad because all we had to do was play a brief game of footsie with our hands.

There are a vast number of different global and historical greeting behaviours. Some you would recognise instantly, some you would understand as variants of greetings you have seen, and others, like the breast suckle, would, one presumes, be new to you. But the identification of particular greetings with particular cultures is often a gross generalisation. Cultures are made up of individuals, and individuals, of course, don't always conform. No culture is monolithic. In England we shake hands ... or do some of us hug, some of us kiss, some of us squirm at any form of human contact? In England we like sarcastic, dry humour ... do we? Do we *all* like sarcasm? Have you met the YouTube comments section? In England, our national dish is fish and chips ... we *all* love that, right? Behaviour within a geographical region can vary between religious groups, generations, genders and regions, as well as things that are harder to define like attitude, mood and (if you believe some of the people who message me) star signs. And yet *we can still* see patterns, trends and clusters. And those clusters tell us things – for example, that some greetings, like the handshake, seem to be winning a popularity contest.

However, there is a big caveat: speaking conclusively on the subject of greeting behaviours worldwide is very hard because peer-reviewed, global or regional studies of greeting diversity don't really exist. For some reason we are lacking large-scale anthropological and ethnographic comparative studies on the subject. It is actually quite surprising: we appear to have a data void. The problem is made worse by the amplification of the small pieces of information we do have, which are often hearsay, based on one individual's fleeting experience or dubious reportage. When outsiders look into a culture, things can easily be misunderstood, lost in translation, performed for the benefit of tourists or exaggerated, exoticised or sexed up. As academics we always say: look at the data, the nuanced hard data and analyses – always. But the research simply isn't there. So why do the French kiss and the English settle for a handshake? Welcome to a bit of a research no-man's-land.

Why the diversity?

The sheer diversity of these greeting rituals can be almost overwhelming. Let us just take one of them, the good old handshake. If you were thinking of the handshake as 'join hands, shake, release', then you're only seeing a tiny part of the story. The handshake comes in endless iterations, and the most common version we use in the West is perhaps the least exciting – the handshake-lite. Many other cultures add another element of touch, from a finger snap to a hand placed on the heart to a nose rub, imbuing a handshake in, say, Ghana with a very different character to one on the Yemeni island of Socotra.

So where does this diversity come from? Many animals show signs of cultural diversity – our old friends the chimps, for instance, appear to differ between groups in terms of how they like to say goodbye[1] – but none come close to the astonishing abundance we see in human culture. We know that this disparity isn't a result of our genetic diversity, because humans actually have quite low genetic diversity compared to other species. I am personally swayed by theories that point to a combination of greater brain capacity, the way in which we form groups and communities, and our adaptability, which allows us to occupy so many different geographical and ecological niches. Once we're separated from other groups of humans by geographical boundaries like mountain ranges or seas, our rituals begin to evolve along different lines, and what starts out as similar (perhaps something like the quick let's-make-up finger-touch that chimps do today) becomes something quite different. Differences might also be developed deliberately, as a way to differentiate between the 'in' group from the 'out' group – as a demonstration, or even symbol, of belonging which is still seen in forms like the Masonic handshake. Mithraism, a secretive Roman cult sometimes thought to have been an early 'sister religion' to Christianity, had an initiation ceremony involving a handshake, and members were known as *syndexioi* ('united by the handshake').[2] You *want* to co-operate more with your own group because it is genetically advantageous; the more you help your own community, the more likely your genes will make it. And to help you do so, you develop more and more specialised habits and rituals, simultaneously increasing bonding with your own group and making it harder to communicate with others from another group. And so cultures run away with themselves and diversify.[3]

Humans are nothing if not paradoxical, though, for even if we are partial to stigmatising outsiders and belonging to a group, we also like to (or, just as often, must) move around and mix together. This cultural blending creates even more diversity. Immigrant communities today often retain some cultural traits from the 'motherland', adopt some of their new country's and create some hybrids of their own. When I was growing up in Birmingham, members of the Yemeni community, who came from a region called Shamir, would talk about a *bakya*. My parents come from a different part of Yemen and we assumed it was Shamiri slang, but their families in Yemen didn't recognise it, neither did their non-Yemeni neighbours. It turns out *bakya* is actually an Arabisation of 'backyard'. What you have here is a 'daughter culture' that is similar but also clearly different, as anyone who's ever tried my (heavily cumin-scented) shepherd's pie would tell you. In some ways what we are talking about is, lo and behold, descent with modification – or evolution, albeit cultural evolution.

Extinction

Of course, a by-product of cultural evolution is extinction, and so the longevity and widespread presence of the hand-shake seems significant. Sure, we can point to a common ancestor and a biological imperative for touch, but why does the culture of *Homo sapiens* feature it so prominently? And why is the specific unit of touch represented by the handshake doing so well? We are very social creatures, and as our social groups grew larger and began to include people we neither knew nor were related to, perhaps the handshake proved to be useful as shorthand: a simple, *quick*, instinctive gesture whose meaning transcended the cultural differences between your valley and the neighbouring one. It is also worth think-ing about the borders which originally promoted cultural diversity: there is a strange balancing act that happens at com-munity boundaries, a necessary equilibrium between conflict and co-operation, depending on which is more advantageous regarding the availability of resources. In order to manage such situations it is useful to have universal gestures that can aid peaceful co-operation, and some anthropologists have hypothesised that this is where the wave originated.[4] Another factor is probably that, as groups got larger and more diverse, elaborate greetings became harder to sustain: some of the extinct salutations seem fantastic but also laborious and time-consuming. It's easy to imagine how some of the more elaborate versions might have died away if you think of how, in a small village, a walk down the street involves stopping to greet the people you pass, whereas in London and New York there are just too many of us. Can you imagine having to stop to perform a greeting ritual with everyone you walk past? To be fair, I've seen stranger things in NYC.

Sadly, linguistic extinction is a concept we're familiar with: of 100,000 or so original human languages, only about 6,000 to 7,000 remain today.[5] Something similar has happened with our gestures, too; we are living amongst the ruins of an enormously diverse range of greetings, rituals and cultures. During my research, I spent a long time looking at historical accounts by explorers and anthropologists who detail a plethora of sometimes fantastic, and always fascinating, greeting behaviour, much of which is now nowhere to be found except in the oral histories of the descendants of the original practitioners or in dusty library vaults.

The cause of these linguistic and cultural extinctions is the technological, and therefore political, advancement of one group at the expense of others – allowing them to spread, exert more influence and eventually dominate. Ten thousand years ago, agriculture was invented, and its advantages for farmers were pretty significant. Aside from revolutionising food security, agriculture allowed humans to come together in larger groups than could be supported by the hunter-gatherer lifestyle, and thus more homogeneity ensued. We can be sure that there were more languages and greeting cultures, almost certainly including handshakes, in existence before the farming expansion than after it. The same is true of colonialism and subsequently globalisation: the technological advancement of the West allowed it to seize territory across the world where European languages and cultures were imposed, causing the extinction of local languages and customs. Sometimes this was a deliberate strategy by the occupying nation, but even in the absence of coercion or even force some people chose to align themselves with the traditions of the new power, seeing it as advantageous for themselves. And today, globalisation and the interconnectedness afforded by modern travel have, I'm sure, been the final nail in the coffin of some of the more unusual greetings.

In all this, the handshake is the English, Spanish or Mandarin of gestures: the lingua franca of powerful and influential countries, commonly understood across vast swathes of the globe. Throughout this chapter, I keep speculating about why the handshake, in particular the style of handshake prominent in the West, has proved more successful than many other units of touch: I suggest that globalisation and the political dominance of hand-shaking nations such as the USA and UK mean that the handshake has dominated over other touch-based greetings, such as, say, I don't know, the penis handshake (keep reading).

The survivors
Hand-cracking, finger-snapping and other variants
The handshake used commonly in the West – the precise choreography of grasp, shake and release – is the scaffolding on which something much more elaborate can be built. In many African countries and regions, including Liberia,Kenya and Ghana, there is a handshake that culminates in a finger snap or click, and Nigeria has one which involves clasping and snapping just the thumbs. The louder the snap the better. It's difficult to master; I have tried to emulate it but my snap at the end … is soundless. I guess failure comes in all shapes and sizes. Outside Africa, an article in 1929 describes an intriguingly similar-sounding greeting in Banks Island, in the Arctic Archipelago, where 'a man locks the middle finger

of his right hand with that of the person he meets and pulls it away with a crack'.[6] The Maasai have a number of different greeting behaviours, including one which is more of a brief palm touch than a handshake. We also see regional variations in angles of the handshake, with diagonal handshakes and vertical clenching common in parts of Africa, while the firmness and length of handshakes might also vary from region to region.

Many of the handshake variants have a performative element that makes the solemn British version look by comparison more like someone's first day in a hot-yoga class than a Cirque de Soleil extravaganza. In Namibia, for example, you might witness a crouch, applause and then a handshake. There is enormous variation in these add-ons: in parts of Ethiopia the handshake comes with a friendly shoulder bump,[7] in other regions of Africa it might also involve a hand on one's inner elbow, and in Greece a hand on one's elbow or a pat on the back. And all over the Middle East, Turkey and in Muslim communities of the Indian subcontinent, a handshake can be accompanied by a hand to the heart.

The hug

The hug is the most significant unit of touch, the gold standard: the amount of surface area covered – and therefore value created, whether you're talking about hormone release or sense receptors being triggered – in the hug is without rival. Hugs can be stand-alone greetings, although it's not unusual to find them combined with a handshake or kiss. As a formalised gesture, we see them in cultures all over the world – but as an expression of familiarity and closeness they are common to us all. As a greeting behaviour, the primary indicator of hugging is not geographical or cultural but familiarity: appropriate, given that most of us have been hugged from the very beginning; we were cradled by our mothers.

La bise

The kiss, known as *la bise* in France, is most commonly associated (in England) with that nation and its touchy-feely ways,[8] but kisses form part of greeting rituals across the world. In Colombia a single kiss is the norm, while the not famously demonstrative Russians do two or three, followed by a hug. Across the Middle East something between two and four kisses is common, and in some parts of Afghanistan it's said they hit the heady heights of *eight* kisses. Interestingly, according to one person I spoke to, the Belgians see anything under three kisses as typical of French bourgeois uptightness and are keen to be seen as more friendly than their Gallic neighbours.

Why some cultures love kissing and others aren't so sure is a difficult one. But the question of why we kiss in the first place is much easier to answer. The kiss is extensively referenced in ancient sources from Homer to St Paul,[9] but I think it is likely to be much older; many of the same arguments and theories that can be put forward about the biological imperative of the handshake can also be put forward about the kiss. After all, biologically it's *touch* that is important in greetings and, like the handshake, the kiss is a unit of touch. As well as our lips being a particularly sensitive part of our body, the mouth is right next to our olfactory organ, so when we place our mouths on or near something it makes it easier for us to pick up any scent-based information about it. It's possible that our ancestors found it informative upon greeting an individual to know how his or her mouth smelt; and, given the choice of mating or hunting with an individual with fewer caries, more teeth, fewer abscesses and less odour, who could blame them?

Not all kisses involve face-to-face contact, of course. Many different hybrids of kisses and handshakes exist, suggesting that the boundaries between different forms of greeting are often more porous than we might imagine. Once a familiar sight, the kiss on the hand is rarely seen in Britain these days – although I have occasionally experienced it, and in his book *One Kiss or Two?* the diplomat Andy Scott mentions that it is still used by men in Austria, Poland and Hungary (always with a female recipient). A gender-neutral version is widely practised in the Middle East, where a kiss of the hands is a sign of respect – two young, unrelated members of the opposite sex wouldn't engage in this, but I have done it myself with older family members and even been on the receiving end if they haven't seen me in a while. In Yemen there is an even more elaborate version, in which you clasp hands, then bring their hand to your mouth for a kiss and they then do the same with your hand. This is often repeated a few times, sometimes culminating in the younger individual then lifting the hand to their forehead. I had quite a lot of trouble nailing the choreography, which was painful to watch. It was blindingly obvious I was raised in Birmingham and not Sana'a.

In parts of Africa like the Congo and in the Middle East, kissing the forehead is a sign of respect, especially when greeting an elder, while the kissing of feet is found in Bangladesh and India. I have also seen this in parts of the Middle East, where a much older relative or mother is greeted by someone kissing their feet; as feet are not considered to be respectful (which is why you might have seen images of Iraqis throwing shoes at statues of Saddam or at US officials in press conferences), to kiss someone's feet in these cultures is a sign of elevated respect and submission.

Noses and foreheads

Like the kiss, the nose rub is a unit of touch found in various geographical locations, and is presumably another form of information-gathering. Sometimes this seems pretty explicit in the structure of the gesture; in one of the most famous, the Maori *hongi*, after a spear is thrown or a weapon raised, the nose and forehead touch, accompanied by deep breathing. The Inuit greeting of 'nose-rubbing' is actually more accurately described as pressing the nose to the skin and inhaling, while in Fiji it is said that people originally preferred sniffing each other. In Oman the nose rub can be accompanied by lots of loud kissing noises made in close succession. The inhabitants of the Gulf Arab states also rub noses, often while shaking hands, and the same practice can be found on the island of Socotra, which, as mentioned, is part of Yemen but closer geographically to Somalia, although the custom isn't found on either mainland.

Forehead-to-forehead touches are often integrated into the handshake, as in parts of the Democratic Republic of the Congo, but not always; on the island of Guam one might witness a right knuckle on the forehead of an elder. On another Pacific island, Tuvalu, as well as in Greenland, the index finger might be pressed on to the forehead three times.

No touching please

Plenty of greetings cultures don't touch at all. There are of course non-touch-based greetings which do not involve hand gestures. In Japan the term for greeting others is *aisatsu*, and it has considerable cultural significance as a sign of respect. Children are taught about it, as are Japanese robots.[10] Bowing (always from the waist) is its most prominent manifestation. Interestingly, avoiding touch doesn't rule out the handshake: traditionally, the Chinese would shake or grasp their own hands as they bowed.[11] Fascinatingly for me, these non-touch greeting behaviours often still involve the hands, as if their importance and symbolism endure, and what we see today is a relic of a hand-based touch greeting. Consider the namaste in India or the *wai* in Thailand, which involve placing the hands together and a small bow.[12] Traditionally, of course, placing the hands together and upwards is thought to signify a connection to the divine; but I do wonder. On a completely different continent, in Angola, a no-touch, hand-based greeting involves two to three quick claps in succession with the hands pointing upwards as if in prayer; and you can also use this gesture to attract attention, like raising a hand in a classroom. There is a tradition in some Muslim cultures of putting the hand on the heart, even without a handshake. It is particularly handy if there is a bit of distance between you and the recipient; in August 2020 I noticed President Macron using it in his visit to Lebanon after the Beirut port blast. His team had clearly thought it through; as a gesture it was both culturally and COVID-appropriate.

Sometimes the custom or taboo against touching is more specific, affecting the relationships between different members of the same community. This is frequently found in religious or cultural practices: many Muslims, like many Orthodox Jews, frown upon (or forbid) the opposite sex touching each other, meaning that greetings which involve touch are not practised between members of the opposite sex who aren't relatives. (This is sometimes incorrectly interpreted by non-Muslims as meaning that women are not allowed to touch men; in fact it applies to both genders, but wouldn't prevent you, for example, from hugging a close blood relative.) It's worth remembering that a lot of cultures are already pretty segregated. I have already explained how I almost never touched a man's hand for many years, but really I didn't have much opportunity to do so within my community: our worship was usually segregated, our meetings were often though not always segregated, my wedding was segregated (I'm now divorced, so perhaps the segregation should have extended to the bride and groom), and parties were almost always segregated. Not all Muslim communities work in this way, but, when I was growing up, mine did. This might all seem very alien to many readers, but conventions governing touch across Western cultures often also divide along gender lines. Spanish men will traditionally kiss women but not each other; middle-aged and older British men or Southern American gentlemen tend to shake hands with each other, whereas a woman might receive a hug or a kiss.

The extinct

A comprehensive account of global historical greeting behaviours would fill a whole series of books, so I have had to be selective here. Which is sad, because extinct greetings really do run the gamut, from urine ceremonies where an individual was showered from head to toe to the presentation of the buttocks.[13] The vast range of greetings that humanity has retained is, as I've said, merely a trace of what we would once have had. This is very much a continuing trend. As I reached out to friends and colleagues around the world to confirm certain practices mentioned in this book, time and again I heard that yes, it did exist, but 'this is an older tradition, it is no longer common'. Some of the now extinct greetings would have provided fascinating anthropological insights into the particular time and place of their creation; others might seem relatively familiar, the predecessors of ones we still use today. It is the unique and, dare I say it, fantastic ones that I want to celebrate here.

The breast suckle

In *Love and Hate* by Irenäus Eibl-Eibesfeldt there is mention of a greeting once found amongst some in the polar region as well as in a village in Papua, Western New Guinea. One takes a brief 'welcoming suck' on the breast of the chief's wife. I have nothing else to say about this. New Guinea, one of the most culturally diverse places on earth, is home to many isolated and distinct tribes and has the greatest linguistic diversity on the planet. So it isn't surprising that it has many fascinating and unusual greeting behaviours; another mentioned by the same author is using one's right hand to point to one's naval and using one's left to squeeze one's nose.

The penis handshake

Irenäus Eibl-Eibesfeldt also describes some Papuan tribes touching the tip of the penis as a greeting. However, the

Australian anthropologist M. J. Meggitt describes an *actual* penis shake; it is performed by the Walbiri tribe in Australia, usually as part of a larger ritual. Meggitt writes:

> When men from another community or tribe arrive for ceremonies, they usually first perform a penis-offering ritual with their hosts. Each visitor approaches each of the seated hosts in turn and lifts the latter's arm. He presses his penis against the host's hand, so that the sub-incised urethra is in full contact with the palm, and then draws the penis firmly along the hand.[14]

Rejection of another man's penis means the man offering his penis has to either fight or flee. To avoid this, the owner of the rejected penis presents his penis to other hosts he knows, in the hope that they will shake it. If they do they are effectively vouching for him, and this usually means he wins the argument and no fight ensues. On the flip side, in accepting the penis they are also declaring that if they can't make a case for the man, they are prepared to fight for him. While 'the penis handshake' is no longer with us, I was reading about it at the same time as dating a left-wing economist, who, confused, asked me if I was sure I wasn't talking about the Bullingdon Club.

The beard-and-pat

The author of a 1929 article describes how 'the Ainus, a race of people on the Island of Saghalien, and the southern Kuriles, have a custom of rubbing their palms together and stroking the beard'.[15] The Ainus are an indigenous people in Japan and the men traditionally had full beards, as they never shaved them after a certain age. I find this handshake incredibly endearing because it reminds me of that child-hood playground game in which one is expected to show dexterity by rubbing the stomach while patting the head with the other hand. It is almost as if the greeting itself is a test of competence! And who as a child didn't pretend that they had a long beard and stroked it repeatedly, as if to chan-nel a wise man deep in thought.

Chest-beating

During his voyage on the *Beagle* Charles Darwin describes a greeting he observed in Tierra del Fuego in the southernmost tip of the South American mainland consisting of three hard slaps to the other person's chest before exposing your own, all while making noises:

> We became good friends – this was shown by the old man patting our breasts & making something like the same noise which people do when feeding chickens – I walked with the old man & this demonstration was repeated between us several times: at last he gave me three hard slaps on the breast & back at the same time, & making most curious noises. – He then bared his bosom for me to return the compliment, which being done, he seemed highly pleased.[16]

It must be said that neither Darwin nor Captain Cook were particularly complimentary about the language of the people they encountered there, and so it is really unclear whether these are 'noises' or whether they were actually words.

Although Darwin seems surprised by it, a casual slap of

the upper arm or back is often part of the handshake repertoire in Europe and North America, while the slapping
of the chest seems reminiscent of the hug's more aggressive
cousin, the 'bro' chest bump.

Captain Cook, nudity and shark's teeth

Fascinating though these stories are, they must be viewed
with caution. On his journeys through the South Pacific,
Captain Cook encountered and described a vast number of
cultures which are now extinct, or which have been largely
assimilated into others. These include two in Tahiti; in one,
wailing and cutting the body with shark's teeth was a form
of greeting, and in the other a woman in Tahiti 'exposed
herself ... naked from the waist downwards'.[17] However, I
did wonder if she might have been flirting with him, but, like
many a scientist, the man was just clueless. Captain Cook,
typical of those who have documented unusual greeting
behaviours (and cultures generally, for that matter), was an
outsider; what's more he was just passing by, and the time he
spent with each culture was very short. His writings make it
clear that he was often unsure of what was really going on
and that much was lost in translation, so it is impossible to
know what the reality of these greetings was.

Continuing with this theme, let's return to the Sentinelese, whom we met at the beginning of the book. There is
a description in a 1993 article in the *Independent* of their
traditional greeting, 'which is to sit in a friend's lap and slap
your right buttock vigorously'.[18] Except that not only do
anthropologists *not* speak Sentinelese, but they have quite
literally barely come into contact with them – they are,
after all, an uncontacted tribe! So how can this 'greeting' be

described with any degree of confidence? The anthropologists might have actually observed mere playfulness; it's also possible that this has been wrongly attributed to the Sentinelese and is instead a description of a different tribe. It might also be hearsay.

Intercultural awkwardness … and who wins

All of this cultural diversity can make for some awkward moments. In 2012 Barack Obama caused a minor diplomatic ripple when he kissed Aung San Suu Kyi, resulting in shock because it broke a taboo against public displays of affection in Myanmar. A Burmese professor of business, Dr Htwe Htwe Theina, wrote to the *Guardian* that the emotions caused by the breach were complex, and not purely negative:

> Shyness (culturally inappropriate way of greeting), admiration (well, every woman from 18 to 80 probably wished it was their cheek on which the Obama kisses had been planted), cheekiness ([her cousin] had to conceal discussion of this 'kiss' talk from her husband who was sitting nearby), surprise (this isn't the usual thing in Burmese culture) and concern (that the media might be critical of this rather intimate greeting).[19]

Similarly, some British sensibilities were mildly outraged by the breach of protocol that occurred when Michelle Obama hugged the Queen (personally, I found it quite endearing). Additionally, the Americans threw a whole pile of tea in some harbour, precisely because they didn't want to follow those rules.

Beyond the world of high-stakes diplomacy, there are many everyday examples of the difficulty we encounter when navigating differences. It's notable that the Obama–Aung San Suu Kyi interaction opens with a number of Western-style handshakes between the two leaders that don't seem to have been controversial, so perhaps at least part of the handshake's international success is due to its relative propriety compared to some of the other tactile examples we've looked at in this chapter, like the kiss. Although one study which documented the responses of American, Saudi and Japanese businesspeople to the handshake found that even with the basic-model handshake there were different perceptions 'regarding acceptable strength, duration, and different types'.[20] It concluded with a recommendation that companies incorporate handshake coaching into their overall training, which sounds almost painfully boring even to me, who wrote a book on the subject.

Sometimes we gain real insight from the clash of cultures: when you have conflicting greeting traditions, which do you pick? My own life is a testament to how confusing it is to navigate cultural differences, rules and taboos. It's strange to see my life reduced to anthropological trends (although why not – I do it to others), but is it really any surprise that someone like me, the child of immigrants, would eventually succumb to the dominant culture's style of salutation? Of course, many of us also try to be culturally sensitive: in parts of the Muslim world, when I am unsure of the level of conservatism adhered to by the person I'm meeting, I will only initiate non-touch greetings, allowing them to lead and mirroring their behaviour. I regularly see diplomats, Western and regional NGO workers and journalists do something similar. Obviously, in that particular context there is strong motivation to build relationships with the people we encounter. And in any case we *are* the minority, succumbing somewhat to local customs.

But, for many, these missed connections aren't about difference and misunderstanding, but about who wins and whose culture comes out on top. A study of the interactions between Tanzanians and Chinese migrants in Tanzania concluded that a refusal on behalf of each group to greet each other had its roots in the 'global material inequalities between China and Africa'; each side suspected the other of using the relationships such a greeting might kindle for manipulative purposes.[21] Then, more often than not, the less powerful culture bows to the more powerful one; sometimes this goes further and legal and political pressure is brought to bear to 'regularise' greeting behaviour – as in the case of an Algerian woman who was denied French citizenship in 2016 because she refused to shake hands with two male officers at the relevant ceremony. The Conseil d'État upheld the denial of citizenship, stating that 'in a place and at a moment that are symbolic, [her behaviour] reveals a lack of assimilation'.[22]

This is clearly cultural assimilation with a stick, sadly something which has all too often been the case. Both historically and today, Christian missionary activity has often included a push to get communities to abandon traditions which were seen as not innately 'Christian' – which in practice meant that they weren't innately Western. (Missionary activity isn't universally Christian by any means, although some of the most famous examples do derive from that religion; Muslim missionaries, depending on their interpretation of religious texts, will often try to get people to stop touching the opposite sex during greetings or kissing another's feet, as it might be seen as prostration.) The anthropologist Monica C. LaBriola describes a typical case of this, when the British came into contact with the *ri-aelōñ-kein* (Marshal Islanders). Missionaries believed that 'complete spiritual conversion would only take place if local customs were also transformed' and set out to change their traditional practices, labour and dress: 'Vital customs such as tattoo ceremonies, dances, food preparation, and medicinal practices were banned. Even the *mejenma* – the *ri-aelōñ-kein* embrace by touching noses – was replaced with the less intimate handshake.'[23]

Of course, it isn't just colonialism, missionaries and/or force which change greeting behaviour; so does globalisation. Soft power is still power. After years of Masai contact with Western culture and tourists, 'a brief handshake, a fist wave, or a fist bump is what the younger generation does today. Unlike the past, when they would reverentially bow their head before the elders and engage in lengthy conversations, today they engage in fleeting salutations. Youngsters use previously unheard terms like *shikamoo* and *papa supai* (Hi) to greet elders.'[24]

Amongst these meetings and conflicts of cultures, the good old handshake – specifically the handshake we see commonly in Western cultures – has come out on top. And it keeps on rising. The handshake's origins might lie deep in our DNA, but the *kind* of handshake we use speaks of the patterns of power and dominance established in our more recent history as a species. Even in the cultures of South and Far East Asia, where traditionally the handshake was absent, it is now frequently used. In a previous chapter, I hypothesised that the handshake's disappearance in these areas was a response to one or more historical epidemics. Perhaps, over the course of centuries, this is simply the handshake working its way back in; it's what it does, and this is a pattern we see repeatedly throughout history. But it is clearly also a response to the West and anglophone countries' influence, and has been for a while. The handshake, and the handshake common in the West, has always existed, but the fact that it is dominant is a testament to power and dominance more than to biology. There's much about the handshake that smacks of egalitarianism; but until we see Liberian finger-snapping in the corridors of Whitehall or Washington DC, we should remember that it often tells a story about imperialism and conquest as well.

4

A Step-by-Step Guide to the Handshake

A survey has shown that 70 per cent of people in the UK are not confident about their hand-shaking technique, a figure that I find astonishing given how natural – even inbuilt – our desire to shake hands seems to be.[1] Perhaps it's down to the general social awkwardness of the Brits, or the messaging of etiquette gurus and business guides which insist on the vital importance of getting it *right*.

It's something of a cliché that you can tell a lot about someone from their handshake, and perfecting the art does seem to be an obsession in some circles. It is said that John F. Kennedy commissioned a study on how to greet world leaders, and in 2010 Chevrolet asked Professor of Psychology Geoffrey Beattie of Manchester University to identify the perfect handshake.[2] He came up with a mathematical formula so extensive that it must be a publicity stunt, while simultaneously identifying twelve very reasonable variables that include eye contact and hand temperature. Here it is:

$$PH = \sqrt{(e2 + ve2)(d2) + (cg + dr)2 + \pi\{(42)(42)\}2 +}$$
$$(vi + t + te)2 + \{(42)(42)\}2$$

(e) is eye contact (1=none; 5=direct) 5; (ve) is verbal greeting (1=totally inappropriate; 5=totally appropriate)

5; (d) is Duchenne smile – smiling in eyes and mouth, plus symmetry on both sides of face, and slower offset (1=totally non-Duchenne smile (false smile); 5=totally Duchenne) 5; (cg) is completeness of grip (1=very incomplete; 5=full) 5; (dr) is dryness of hand (1=damp; 5=dry) 4; (s) is strength (1= weak; 5=strong) 3; (p) is position of hand (1=back towards own body; 5=other person's bodily zone) 3; (vi) is vigour (1=too low/too high; 5=mid) 3; (t) is temperature of hands (1=too cold/too hot; 5=mid) 3; (te) is texture of hands (5=mid; 1=too rough/too smooth) 3; (c) is control (1=low; 5=high) 3; (du) is duration (1= brief; 5=long) 3.

Chevrolet apparently included a 'simplified version' of Beattie's formula in their training material, while it was reported in 2007 that Yale University was offering lessons in 'proper hand-shaking technique' to graduate students.[3] Presumably these measures were based on the well-established idea that, particularly in a professional setting, a 'good' handshake is essential; as a student advisor at Simon Fraser University in Canada put it, the handshake is 'still the best way to make a strong impression in a business and employment setting'.[4] Really? Not a smile, not intelligent conversation, not a warm, emotionally literate manner … not, I don't know, appropriate qualifications and an impressive CV?

I am, of course, an advocate of the handshake. But I don't think it is about 'proper technique' – which, in any case, often seems to translate as a barely disguised power play. Having said that, I will now join the 'auspicious' ranks of business gurus and etiquette twats everywhere by taking you through a step-by-step guide to the handshake. But, as you can probably tell, this will be less prim-and-proper-by-way-of-finishing-school and more a radical anthropologist's view. I should probably add a disclaimer at this point: my only qualification for writing this guide is that I am a human adult. This is the Delia Smith 'How-to-boil-an-egg' recipe for handshakes.

Setting the scene

The handshake is no contest

So how do you conduct a handshake? Think of what Donald Trump would do. Are you imagining it? OK, now do the opposite. I could honestly end the chapter here; the handshake is about civility, symmetry, egalitarianism and warmth, and if you see it as an arena in which to 'one-up' your 'opponent' you have fundamentally misunderstood what the gesture is about.

This is (one of) the problems with much of the business and etiquette literature on the subject: the identification of the handshake as a way to assert yourself at the expense of the other person. As *Business Etiquette: Gaining That Extra Edge* puts it, 'Knowing how to shake hands well is essential for people who want that upper hand.'[5] Similarly, the intention of etiquette coaches appears to be not to help people overcome the kind of social anxiety that leads to avoidable fumbling and embarrassment, but to reinforce a set way of doing things which distinguishes an elite from the uninformed masses. They are there not to help people but to separate them. I'm an archaeologist, I like very old things – and I'm telling you that this is outdated and you need to move on. Etiquette coaches, proselytising elitism, are not the gatekeepers of the handshake, because the handshake is not exclusionary.

So, first and foremost, remember that the handshake isn't about power or status, and to treat it as such is to subvert its very nature. There were reports in 1863 in England of a practice whereby some 'fine ladies' would only offer two fingers in a handshake to those they saw as being beneath them:

> ... they use this means to express the feeling of their own importance, and also to convey to the person whom they confer this doubtful honour a proper sense of the distance that separates them ... and from the affable smile with which they accompany the gesture it is evident that they seriously believe those kind of people must be pleased and proud to have this mark of condescension shown them.

Not surprisingly, those on the receiving end didn't appreciate the 'implication of inferiority', and some even returned the insult. Basically, don't be a 'fine lady'.[6]

Are you ill?
It goes without saying that, until COVID-19 is under control, keep your mittens to yourself. And generally, if you have so much as a sniffle the truly courteous thing is to avoid a handshake entirely (you can find the next-best alternative in the Epilogue). B. Pachter, a career coach, 'recommends using medication to suppress the signs of illness before the meeting or event and "discreetly" using hand sanitizer

before shaking someone's hand. She goes so far as to state that if you witness someone sneeze into their hand and then reach out for a handshake, as a prudent businessperson you should take their hand and then immediately go to the wash-room and sanitize.'[7] That's madness!

Are you ready and are they ready?

Do they want to shake hands? As a gesture and form of body language, the handshake is about symmetry and reciprocity, so extend that to cultural and social sensitivities as well. If you suspect that your partner doesn't want to shake hands, hang back briefly and let them lead, mirroring their actions.

First impressions *do* count; however, they aren't created by the angle of your handshake but by being respectful, nice and warm. So if you both want to go ahead, smile, give a verbal greeting, if possible stand up if they are standing, and try to face them (including with your feet) as if your whole body is engaging with them. A handshake is a chance to forge a connection with another person so, if you can, give them a few moments of your time, make eye contact and generally convey the impression of giving a damn. Never offer a less-than-clean and, ideally, warm hand. If your hand is clammy, wipe it discreetly on your clothing, the tablecloth or some nearby curtains. If you have time, take your gloves off.

The execution

Shaking hands the right way

Use your right hand (if you – and they – can). The left hand seems to be almost universally taboo (or at the very least, less preferred), left-handed handshakes such as the Scouts' being an exception to the rule.[8] The positive symbolism associated with the right hand, and conversely, the negative symbolism associated with the left hand, is very deeply rooted in our history. In the Islamic tradition, the right hand is clean and the left unclean: amongst religious communities, you use your left for things like going to the toilet and your right for eating. This originated in a world where there was little soap, sometimes even water, so it wasn't a bad system, although today it means that I still cannot use a fork in my left hand – I am essentially left-side illiterate. This analogy between the right side and purity is extended to a right–left moral divide found not just in Islam but numerous other cultures: in Christianity Jesus sits at God's right hand, while the Balinese also associate good with the right side and evil with the left.[9] The anthropologist Ethel J. Alpenfels speculated that perhaps the custom of men buttoning to the right and women to the left harks back to these associations. (Ladies, thanks to misogyny, even your coat is judging you.)

Why this preference for the right over the left? It is unclear, although anthropologically it is probably no coincidence that left-handedness is relatively rare: globally, only about 10 per cent of people are left-handed, and we aren't alone in this – Neanderthals too were by and large righties. The right, as we see it, is 'normal' and therefore good. So it is no surprise that it is the right one of these hugely significant appendages which partakes in the handshake. As a serious academic and researcher I would love to dismiss the prejudice against left-handers as nonsense ... but I have suddenly realised that the overwhelming majority of my exes are left-handed, so perhaps there is something in this. Anyway, unless there's a good reason not to, use your right hand.

Grip

Grip is in many ways the most contentious aspect of handshake etiquette. Business manuals often place emphasis on the importance of 'a firm handshake' as a way of impressing the recipient, and – surprising though it is – it seems there is some justification for this theory. Grip strength is quite fashionable in medical research as an indicator of general health and longevity, and a study by *The Lancet* suggests that 'reduced muscular strength, as measured by grip strength, has been associated with an increased risk of … mortality' (so, quite a bit worse than not landing that deal).[10] A study of two indigenous groups, the Yali (from New Guinea) and the Hadza (from Tanzania), concluded that 'greater hand grip strength is associated with better hunting outcomes among Hadza males' (although there wasn't a similar correlation found amongst the Yali).[11] Historically, at least, it might well be that the handshake, or specifically the grip part of it, is essentially a way of testing each other's fitness – from an evolutionary perspective, something that is useful to know when meeting another individual.

If this is indeed true, it provides an exasperating perspective on gender relations in the workplace. There is some exploratory research that suggests that 'the relationship between a firm handshake and interview ratings may be stronger for women than for men',[12] and, perhaps relatedly, women are often counselled to make sure their handshake is strong in order to succeed and impress in the workplace.

As the executive coach Carol Kinsey Goman notes, 'good' handshakes ('firm, web-to-web, palm-to-palm') are 'especially important for females in the workplace – because *women with firm handshakes are evaluated as positively as men*' (emphasis in original). Goman goes on to provide eleven tips for women shaking hands in the workplace, including: 'Shake hands firmly. Women with a firm handshake make a more favourable impression and are judged to be confident and assertive.'[13] The problem, of course, is that in many cases women will just naturally have less powerful grips, and the assessment of the 'female' handshake as inadequate and unimpressive appears to be based on good old patriarchal values, in which the masculinised standard is *the* standard. Might this even go back to an outmoded need to see how good other people are at hunting? Should women bother to match the crushing grip of their male colleague, or is theirs perfect as it is? This obsession with grip strength does start to feel a bit like mine-is-bigger-/stronger-than-yours willy-waving.[14]

My own perspective is that – within normal parameters of pressure – a range of grip strengths is acceptable. Generally, it is best to avoid behaving like someone trying to open a bottle that just won't give. As a guide published in 1877 put it, 'A gentleman who rudely presses the hand offered him in salutation, or too violently shakes it, ought never to have an opportunity to repeat his offense.'[15] Hear, hear.

Choreography

And so it culminates in the dance. Stretch your palm out, angle it downwards at a forty-five-degree angle, with the thumb pointing upwards. Oddly, not everyone indulges in the 'shake' or 'pump' part of the handshake; sometimes you just get a squeeze and that's it. I find I usually do just one pump, which on reflection does feel a bit like a vertical flick. Interestingly, in parts of the Middle East, what some lack in grip strength they make up for in the length of the pumping.

There's no right length, number of times to do it, or even agreed distance (height) to move the hands; ideally, just make the handshake long enough so that the person feels seen. But whatever your basic practice is, considerably more is acceptable if you are, for instance, congratulating someone or very excited. The only rule, really, is to read the room, so you don't end up energetically pumping the whole arm of a bemused neighbour who just popped round to see if they could borrow some sugar.

Release
Then release. You will probably know when. Generally it is best if you aren't hanging on until the other person starts planning their exit strategy. But what if it all goes wrong? Do you insist on a rewind and replay, or quietly back away? In instances like this – and just generally for people with handshake-induced social anxiety – it is worth remembering the purpose of the handshake. It isn't about technique as much as it is about intention. Many of the things which 'guides' tell you matter about handshakes in fact don't matter, especially if you are respectful and warm in your general demeanour. Don't obsess about it and remember that the handshake is just one step in a sequence; it is supposed to get you to friendly chatter or help you exit from it, it just book-ends an interaction with another human. A disastrous handshake is something to chat and joke about. Get in with a

smile and some warmth, then get out of that paw exchange. The handshake is not the end game. Human connection is. So there it is. That is how you shake hands. God speed.

5

The Hand of Destiny: History's Best Handshakes

For a gesture which lacks the cinematic glamour of the kiss, the effortless cool of the high five or the thrilling drama of the punch on the nose, the handshake has had a surprisingly frequent ringside seat in the historical record.

In order to show the power of the handshake when it goes right, I have scoured the history books (and my memory) and selected some of the most successful handshakes of the modern era, from all the times we thought we had solved a world problem with a handshake to the photo-op aimed at changing taboos. These were not relatable handshakes: they were often affairs of state, they were steeped in symbolism and meaning, they were iconic. In fact, in most of these cases the handshake itself was a photo-op, orchestrated, choreo-graphed and performed not just for the participants but also for the viewing public. Most of us will never undertake a handshake so imbued with significance.

So, in no particular order of importance, let's take a look at history and culture through the lens of significant handshakes. Dare I say it, it's a deliciously informative sight-seeing hike through history.

The Handshake

Princess Diana and an unnamed AIDS patient

> 'You can shake their hands ... heaven knows they need it.' (Princess Diana)

This is one of my favourite handshakes of all time; it was, in many ways, revolutionary. In 1987, at the height of the AIDS epidemic, the general public believed that you could become HIV-positive simply by touching someone. As a result, people were terrified of anyone carrying the virus, and misinformation resulted in an almost unbearable level of stigma and discriminatory policy; many medical professionals working with HIV-positive patients did not reveal what they were doing to family, friends and even colleagues. Frenzied tabloid headlines from the time included 'Britain threatened by gay virus plague' in the *Mail on Sunday* and 'I'd shoot my son if he has AIDS' in the *Sun*.[1] In 1985 an *LA Times* poll showed that 50 per cent of those asked favoured quarantining HIV patients.[2]

Princess Diana visited the first purpose-built HIV unit, based at London's Middlesex Hospital. Initially, patients refused to shake her hand in front of the cameras because of the negative coverage of the time. Eventually one male patient, who was dying, agreed. For Princess Diana to shake his hand without gloves was one of the simplest yet most disruptive acts of social justice by a privileged individual in living memory: a handshake that led by example, helped to shatter the shame surrounding the disease and revealed the radical power of simply touching another human being. A nurse from the unit, John O'Reily, thought it showed 'that she cared because she shook everybody's hand'.[3] Diana went on to repeat these handshakes many times over the years.

Princess Diana, more than most public figures of the time, knew about the power of images to influence public opinion. In the words of her son, Prince Harry: 'She knew exactly what she was doing.' She was leading by example.

Special mention: the Biden–Harris handshake substitute

On 8 November 2020 former Vice President Joe Biden and Senator Kamala Harris were declared the winners of the US presidential race. Their win represented a number of firsts and they received more votes than any presidential ticket in history. At just after 8 p.m. EST in Delaware, Harris gave an electrifying speech and then introduced Biden, who, about to become the oldest president in US history, ran on to the stage somewhat in the style of a UFC fighter and greeted Harris with a double fist bump.

This was not a handshake, but in the age of COVID-19, it was. And to me, it's another reminder of how a handshake (or non-handshake) can speak a thousand words. We know for sure that, given the Biden campaign's concern with responsible COVID optics and accurate scientific messaging, a handshake between them would have been explicitly off the table. Like Princess Diana, they were interested in leading by example. In any case, I'll be damned if I don't include the fist bump that ended the Trump presidency and celebrated the first female, Black and Indian-American vice president. This is the handshake of our plague-infested but changing time.

The Cold War: Reagan and Gorbachev

In Geneva, on 19 November 1985, US President Ronald Reagan and USSR leader Mikhail Gorbachev shook hands, spelling the beginning of the end of the Cold War. Certainly a 'handshake that changed history' on that basis alone, it's also seen as a testament to the power of Swiss diplomacy,[4] and (by me) as revealing how the background setting can be almost as important as the gesture itself.

The location for a handshake between the world's two enemy superpowers – a deeply symbolic occasion – was indeed a difficult decision. It couldn't be left to another superpower to host and broker the deal, as is often the case: there were no other superpowers. It would be seen as capitulation for one of the superpowers to be hosted by the other, a sign of weakness for the 'away team'. Most of the rest of the world had aligned with one power or the other, so there was very little neutral territory. Switzerland was the only possible location for this handshake, and so it was amongst the lakes and cuckoo clocks of Europe's most unobjectionable country that the slow thawing of geopolitical relations began.

This handshake was the first of many regularly on-display handshakes during the years of negotiations and treaties that followed. It is also a reminder, of course, that one handshake does not effectively end forty years of hostilities and ideological conflict; it's also a sign of the unique flexibility of the handshake that it can mark both a beginning and an end.

The 1964 Civil Rights Act: Martin Luther King and Lyndon Johnson

This handshake stands out for its unusual choreography. President Lyndon Johnson signed the Civil Rights Act while seated, surrounded, even crowded by standing men, including the Reverend Martin Luther King. Immediately after signing, and while still seated, he turned to Martin Luther King, simultaneously passed him one of the seventy-two pens used to sign the Act – and shook his hand. The unstudied immediateness of the gesture can be read as eagerness, as if signifying 'it's about time'. It's one of the messiest and least choreographed of the famous handshakes, perhaps because it was so overdue. It took place on 2 July 1964. A year later the Voting Rights Act, which protected the voting rights of racial minorities, was signed. This time, the set-up was much more in line what you might expect: after signing, Johnson actually stood up before he shook the Reverend's hand, underlining the haste of the previous occasion.[5]

Egypt and Israel: Anwar Sadat and Menachem Begin

26 March 1979 saw the formal signing of the Camp David Accords, the peace treaty between Egypt and Israel which ended thirty years of war and hostilities. It was conducted on the South Lawn of the White House, and featured a handshake between Egyptian President Anwar Sadat and Prime Minister Menachem Begin of Israel, both of whom had been made Nobel Peace Laureates after the negotiation of the treaty the previous year. But, historic though it was in its own right, this handshake is also notable for the presence of a third figure: US President Jimmy Carter. Carter had played a pivotal role in the negotiation of the treaty, and he stands front and centre over the handshake, his hands (perhaps awkwardly) interlocked with those of Sadat and Begin, as if to show this celebration is as much

about the peacemaker as it is about the peace. Similarly, on 13 September 1993, we find Bill Clinton front and centre, arms spread in paternal embrace, standing between the Palestinian leader Yasser Arafat and the Israeli leader Yitzhak Rabin as they shake hands after signing the Oslo Accords, emphasising America's role in orchestrating and delivering the (ultimately failed) peace.

The three-way handshake is a relatively rare beast, although one did take place at the 1945 Yalta Conference between Churchill, Roosevelt and Stalin. In it, a smiling Roosevelt stands between the more subdued British and Russian leaders, forming the central link in a chain of shaken hands. It looks uncomfortable – perhaps not surprisingly, given that relations between the wary allies were already beginning to sour.

Malcolm X and Martin Luther King

Malcolm X and Martin Luther King were both titans of the African American Struggle, whose views on how to achieve racial equality in the USA didn't always align (to put it mildly).[6]

Their views differed on the merits of racial integration, whether white people could join the movement, and on the role which violence might play in the fight for equality. But Malcolm X's views changed over time. In the last part of his life he left the Nation of Islam and converted to Orthodox Islam; on the Hajj pilgrimage in April 1964, he reflected on how moved he was to pray and eat with Muslims of all colours. The result was an ideological shift on race, bringing him closer to the views of Martin Luther King.

Malcolm X had attempted to meet King before, but was seen as too radical by the moderate wing of the Civil Rights Movement. They didn't reply to his requests. But then on 25March 1964, having left the Nation of Islam and just before setting out on the pilgrimage that would transform his thinking, he found himself watching a Senate hearing about segregation. Martin Luther King was also in attendance. Malcolm approached him, shook hands and said: 'I'm throwing myself into the heart of the civil rights struggle.' However, a second meeting between the two men planned for February 1965 never happened, after King and others were arrested in Selma. On 21 February, Malcolm X was assassinated.

That one face-to-face meeting, right at the beginning of Malcolm X's ideological shift and lasting a mere few moments, was the only time these two men ever met. Of all the handshakes featured here, this is the only one which for me is a lament. What would have happened if the meeting of minds it marked was allowed to reach fruition? These were two of the most gifted orators the USA had ever seen, who reached the highest heights as activists. They came from different centres of gravity, poised on the edge of a collaboration that would have been far greater than the (considerable) sum of its parts. To reflect on what this handshake could have led to is to undergo a gut punch.[7]

England and Ireland: Queen Elizabeth II and Martin McGuinness

One of the better-known meanings of the handshake is 'let bygones be bygones', a connotation it also appears to have for chimps. And it's hard to think of a better example of a relationship riddled with potential sources of whatever the opposite of bygones is than the one between the IRA and the British state – which makes the 2012 handshake between Queen Elizabeth II and ex-IRA leader (then Deputy Leader of Sinn Féin) Martin McGuinness a prime example of this genre. After all, there was quite a lot to forgive, including the IRA's assassination of Lord Mountbatten, the Queen's second cousin once removed, in 1979 and the brutal history of British rule, not to mention the IRA's extensive list of grievances with regards to Northern Ireland. McGuinness recalls: 'Whenever I met with Queen Elizabeth, she never asked me to apologise for anything and I didn't ask her to apologise for anything.'[8]

The lasting peace achieved in Northern Ireland once seemed impossible; it is a remarkable accomplishment, and a ray of hope for other bitter and long-standing conflicts across the globe. This was a handshake – between two people who'd suffered personally as a result of the struggle – not to signal an intention to make a peace deal but to further reinforce the steadfastness and success of one. Long may it continue.

Nelson Mandela and South African rugby captain Francois Pienaar

Rugby during apartheid was a white Afrikaans sport and the South African national team, the Springboks, became a symbol of the racist regime. When apartheid finally ended there were very loud calls from Black South Africans to get rid of the Springboks and change the symbol. In 1995

Nelson Mandela, the newly elected president, was in many Afrikaners' minds a terrorist. They feared what a Black man who had been imprisoned for twenty-seven years might do to them in revenge.

And then Nelson Mandela attended the Rugby World Cup, held in Johannesburg, wearing a green Springbok jersey and cap and the team captain's number on his back. The captain, Francois Pienaar, describes how the scene was so emotional that he couldn't sing the national anthem because he knew he would cry. The crowd of 63,000, of whom 62,000 were white, were stunned and began chanting 'Nelson, Nelson'. It was a masterclass in racial healing, conveying wordlessly the significance of Mandela's message of unity rather than retaliation.

South Africa won, beating New Zealand, and on the podium Nelson Mandela shook Francois Pienaar's hand and handed him the trophy. Pienaar recalls:

> I still can't believe to this day that he said ... 'thank you Francois for what you have done for this country'. I wanted to jump over and give him a hug but I said to him, 'no sir, thank you for what you've done for this country' because if he didn't ... tell the ANC and the black people in South Africa that this is our team, they're playing for us, we're one team, we're one country, embrace them, then we wouldn't have had the support we've had.[9]

Sport is rarely just sport: it can be about politics, social division, tribalism, healing – and it can be excellent PR. Mandela and Pienaar's handshake was perfectly choreographed, carefully considered down to Mandela's uniform, and the win a stroke of much-needed good luck. Consolidated at the moment of the handshake, these elements created one of the most iconic images of racial unity and healing.

6

The Hand of Doom: History's
Worst Handshakes

If you've just finished the previous chapter, you're probably feeling pretty good about the handshake: the little gesture that merrily travelled the world and twentieth-century history, righting wrongs and ending wars. But that's only half the story – and in this chapter we'll address what happens when handshakes go wrong, from awkward near-misses to cultural faux pas, deliberate snubs and – in the case of the unfortunate President McKinley – the immediate demise of one of the protagonists. And that's not even the worst in the list.

If the power of the handshake is in the symbolic unity it projects to observers, then a handshake that goes wrong tells a different, but no less powerful, story. Most of the handshakes described in this chapter are would-be-handshakes which never quite happened. Some were intentional snubs, some unintentional, but all are exercises in awkwardness, embarrassment and sometimes actual insult.

So, what does it mean to refuse a handshake, or to be snubbed? In both social psychology and cultural anthropology, the principle of reciprocity – exchanging one thing for another of roughly equal value, whether trading vegetables for grain or repaying a compliment received with one given – is understood to help us develop social relationships. In fact, the French anthropologist Marcel Mauss says that it is one of the rocks 'on which societies are built'.[1] Importantly, reciprocity works both ways: a positive action triggers a positive action in return (you stacked the dishwasher, so I'll make you a cup of tea), but a negative one triggers a retaliation, as in the biblical *lex talionis*, or 'an eye for an eye'. From bartering to politics to relationships, our understanding of the importance of returning like for like is deeply baked into our culture and psychology. A somewhat bleak concept in psychology, social exchange theory, suggests that humans are very often motivated by a kind of social cost-benefit analysis: we invest more in relationships when we're sure that what we're giving will be reciprocated, but let them die away when we feel short-changed.[2]

I am convinced that the whole business of shaking hands is so natural to humans, and our understanding of the significance and value of the handshake so inbuilt, that to *refuse* to shake hands, especially in public, is to make a more psychologically and socially meaningful statement than simply half-heartedly going along with it. Therefore handshake snubs are drama-laden, they are the stuff of sexual betrayal, diplomatic incident, murder and full-on social meltdown. You can't look away.

The USA, China and a tale of two bad handshakes

In 1972 President Nixon got on a plane to China, the first step of a diplomatic mission that ended twenty-five years of pin-drop silence between the two nations. On the tarmac, Nixon was met by the Chinese premier, Zhou Enlai. Recalling the moment, Nixon said: 'As I came down the ramp, Zhou began to applaud. I returned the gesture, and then, as I reached the bottom step, I stretched out my hand to Zhou. When he took it, it was more than a handshake. We both knew that it marked a turning point in history.' For his own part, Zhou Enlai told Nixon: 'Your handshake came over the vastest ocean in the world – twenty-five years of no communication.' Seven months after Nixon had secretly sent Henry Kissinger to Beijing to start negotiations, 'the doors had swung open on a new policy of dialogue between China and the US'.[3]

The handshake gave a competitive advantage to the USA in the Cold War, driving a wedge between the erstwhile allies China and Russia; but, equally importantly, it exorcised the memory of 1954, when at the Geneva Conference Zhou Enlai had offered his hand to Secretary of State John Foster Dulles and had been snubbed. Some have argued that this helped sour relations for two decades.

So why, I hear you asking, is the 1972 handshake in the fails list? On the surface it would appear to have been a resounding success, especially when compared to the 1954 disaster. Perhaps; but these handshakes are part of a package. You can't understand one without the other, even twenty-two years apart: collectively, they show the impact of a handshake snub at the highest level of diplomacy. But second, I think the 1972 handshake may deserve a place here on its own merit because, when you look a little closer, it might have been a snub itself. After all, Zhou was the premier, but he was not the leader of the People's Republic of China, who was Chairman Mao Zedong. Mao would normally go to meet important heads of state, and yet Nixon, the leader of one of the two superpowers, crosses an ocean after two decades of silence – and Mao sends his deputy to greet him. In the high-stakes, high-status game of international diplomacy, it is hard to believe that the American delegation didn't notice this. It's possible that the meaning was actually more simple: Mao was very ill at the time, something the Chinese were keen to keep from the Americans. But even so, it goes to show that, as much as this handshake was a huge international relations success, the story behind it was far from straightforward, just as the relationship between the two countries remained far from trusting. For all its success, the 1972 handshake was not quite the gestural antonym of the 1954 snub.

Obama, Kenny and American–Irish awkwardness

This is a case study in awkward, one of the most relatable and amusing of the handshake disasters on the list. On St Patrick's Day in 2015, Irish Prime Minister Enda Kenny and President Barak Obama are sitting in the White House. In front of the cameras, Kenny extends his hand, ready for the handshake photo-op which is surely on its way. But Obama doesn't see it, and starts speaking to the press: 'Well, it is a great pleasure to once again welcome my good friend …' Kenny looks down at his lonely hand (the hand of Obama's 'good friend'). He spreads his fingers nervously. What to do with your hand? How to save your dignity? We have all been there, Enda, we have all been there – though rarely in the Oval Office with the world's media watching.

However unintentional it was, I can't help thinking that this snub raises an important point about reciprocity and status: would it have occurred the other way around? Would the same thing have happened between, say, George Bush and Tony Blair at the time of the Second Gulf War, when the Americans desperately needed British support? Unintentional snubs might be accidental – but they are still a betrayal of the principle of reciprocity, and so they still cause embarrassment and social discomfort. Both parties understand this, and so if one party isn't paying enough attention to avoid an accidental snub, it suggests an imbalance of power.

Adolf Hitler and Neville Chamberlain

This is truly one of the best examples of a handshake that didn't age well. On 30 September 1938, the German dictator Adolf Hitler and British Prime Minister Neville Chamberlain shook hands on the day of the Munich Agreement, effectively sealing the fate of Czechoslovakia in exchange for what Chamberlain hoped would be the end of German expansionism in Europe. It was a highly lauded handshake at the time and was celebrated with a vast outpouring of hope and joy by the British public, enormously relieved at the thought of 'peace in our time'. But – as we all know – Hitler broke the Munich Agreement, and the handshake was recast as the definition of an empty gesture.

A disaster at the time, the Munich handshake has had an afterlife as a symbol of appeasement, entering the political zeitgeist as a sort of meme, shorthand for a public figure betraying their principles. When Obama met Raúl Castro briefly at Nelson Mandela's funeral in 2013 and shook his hand, Senator John McCain's response was a terse 'Neville Chamberlain shook hands with Hitler'. Some handshakes might start their lives in the previous chapter, but as their consequences come to fruition they end up very firmly in this one.

Hitler, Jesse Owens … and Roosevelt

Held under Nazi rule, the 1936 Berlin Olympics began with a heated international discussion about a possible boycott, and have lived on in our collective memory as a famous example of an egregious handshake snub. The African American athlete Jesse Owens won four gold medals – the first time an American won so many at a single Olympics – only to find that Hitler refused to shake his hand. That is the story; however, the reality turns out to be somewhat more complicated. On the first day of the Olympics, Hitler shook the hands of the German and some Finnish gold medallists and then left the stadium before Cornelius Johnson, an African American, won his. Hitler was reprimanded by the head of the International Olympic Committee, who told him he had to shake hands with all gold medallists or none. Hitler opted for the latter. Some accounts have Hitler waving at Owens instead (or more, jarringly, giving him a small Nazi salute).

Whatever the exact nature of what happened, the headline seems clear: it was a nasty, public rejection by a racist, insecure world leader unable to accept that Black American athletes had beaten his 'master race'. Nazis bad, Americans good. But what I find fascinating about this non-handshake is what Jesse Owens said about it: 'Hitler didn't snub me – it was [Roosevelt] who snubbed me. The president didn't even send me a telegram.'[4] President Roosevelt only invited white Olympians to the White House in 1936. While in Germany, Owens stayed in a hotel with white athletes, a basic human right which was not afforded to him in much of his own country. Back in New York there was a parade and then a reception in his honour to celebrate his wins. But to get to his own reception in the Waldorf Astoria, he had to take the service lift because as a Black man he was banned from using the Waldorf's main entrance. Popular culture has focused on the foreign snub and the convenient Nazi villain, but for African American athletes the picture was more complex and sinister.[5]

Donald Trump and … just about everybody

The handshakes between President Donald Trump and his various … let's just call them 'opponents' are legend-ary. From his lengthy struggles with a dogged Emmanuel Macron to the unnecessary hand-crushing of a puzzled Shinzo Abe, they are something to behold. *The Atlantic* declared: 'TWENTY-NINE SECONDS. That's how long …', the *Independent* brought in body-language experts, CNN did a second-by-second play-by-play and the rest of us watched in disbelief. These handshakes have been analysed to death, but I think all the hours of careful examination by experts can be summarised thus: they are the PG-13 version of dick-swinging. At the risk of pointing out the obvious, they are not exactly in keeping with the reciprocal spirit of handshakes – when you won't let go and keep dragging your partner's hand towards you like an old rag doll, it is less about shaking someone's hand and more about taking it hostage.

History will tell how much of a disservice the Trump family did to the world by not sending him to therapy – and a finishing school. However, his bizarre 'uncouth' handshakes do provide a fascinating insight into his (ahem) unique psychology, in which there are only winners and losers, and friendship and co-operation are for idiots. *The Atlantic* put it well, talking about an exchange with Macron: 'It was also one of many, many times that the current American president attempted to treat the handshake as a power play in miniature.'[6]

Bone-crushing handshakes are hardly unusual from tedious men, but Trump's behaviour as preposterous-hand-shaker-in-chief seems to underline the extent to which he is an outlier, in general decorum as in everything else. When, in October 2016, Donald Trump and Hillary Clinton did not shake hands in the third televised debate,[7] it was the first time that this long-held tradition had been abandoned: a symbolic starting pistol for a new era of incivility and toxic public discourse. It should be noted that during the 2020 presidential debates against Joe Biden (or at least the ones that Trump turned up for), the COVID-19 pandemic served as an excuse for the two men to not shake hands – a good thing, given that the sitting president was possibly infected with the virus at the first one.[8]

Boris Johnson's infamous COVID-19 hand-shaking

This leads us neatly on to British Prime Minister Boris Johnson, who in the early days of the pandemic and against the advice of public-health officials declared that he wasn't giving up handshakes. At a press conference, standing next to a slightly agonised-looking government health advisor, he announced that he had met some COVID patients in hospital: 'I shook hands with everybody, you'll be pleased to know.' Many of us were not pleased; in the following days, even the apolitical morning-show host Phillip Schofield tried to avoid the PM's handshake as Boris doubled down on his risky behaviour. A few weeks later, in a striking example of leading by (bad) example, he was in the ICU with COVID.

Of course, there's no way of knowing for sure if he contracted COVID-19 as a result of not practising handshake abstinence, but his handshakes were a remarkable PR exercise in cause and effect.

John Terry and Wayne Bridge: sex, scandal and football

Whether on the pitch or across the net, handshakes and good sportsmanship quite literally go hand in hand. Most examples of snubbed handshakes in sport are due to two reasons (or a combination of both): politics and racism. There is, however, a famous outlier that stemmed from much more intimate reasons. John Terry and Wayne Bridge were English footballers, friends and, at various times, teammates. John Terry was a superstar, one of the most powerful English footballers of his day, and captain of both England and Chelsea. Wayne Bridge (and his fiancée Vanessa Perroncel) was happy enough to be in his orbit.

Bridge moved from Chelsea to Manchester City in 2009, and his relationship with Perroncel fell apart. Then Terry got a super-injunction from a High Court judge against the press, gagging them from reporting a story about his private life. When it was overturned, the headlines erupted, accusing him of cheating on his wife during a four-month affair with ... Perroncel. The British tabloids, famous for their feeding frenzies on a good day, let alone when a celebrity slighted them by attempting a gagging order, were now on acid and out for revenge. Bridge was inundated with messages of support from footballers; some went as far as wearing shirts with 'Team Bridge' on them. Terry's wife left for Dubai with their children ... and apparently half of England's paparazzi. Terry's reputation nosedived and he was stripped of his captainship of the national team. Adding to the drama was a fast-approaching Chelsea–Manchester City game and, as the scandal became something of a national fixation, bookies began taking bets on whether they would shake hands. At the match, Terry extended his hand and Wayne walked past and ignored it. City won their first game at the Chelsea grounds in seventeen years.

Of course, the main problem with this piquant story of sex and revenge is that Vanessa Perroncel denies all of it, and eight months later the *News of the World* issued her with an apology. Terry regained his captainship, but Bridges' career fizzled; as he reflected years later, 'The most disappointing aspect of it all is that I'm probably more famous for not shaking someone's hand than I am for playing football. I get abuse walking down the street. I still don't think anyone knows the full story.'[9]

Sex and handshakes don't normally go together (it's not the done thing to shake hands after orgasms). I know of no other handshake story that involves alleged steamy affairs, jilted lovers, a scandal and an obsessed nation, so I think this handshake definitely earns its place on this list. But I do feel a bit dirty for including something so salacious and quite possibly baseless ... and for not hating the research into it.

Castro and Obama

The history of handshakes between Raúl Castro and Barack Obama warrants a book of its own, their troubled back-story and the heated discussion of any hand-to-hand contact between the two men being symbolic of the rocky relationship between Cuba and the USA.

We've already discussed the handshake at Nelson Mandela's funeral in 2013. There was a 'legacy handshake' in Panama which aimed to mark a thawing of relations in 2015, which was very unpopular with Republicans. But my favourite Castro–Obama handshake technically wasn't really a handshake at all, it was an unchoreographed mess. A year after the Panama handshake, during a joint press conference in Havana, Castro morphed a would-be handshake into something quite peculiar. He took Obama's wrist and lifted it above his head, presumably intending, if one assumes no malice, a sort of 'over-the-head victorious hand-in-hand posture'. However, if one does assume malice, it was an attempt to force the kind of over-the-head arm salute which is familiar from communist iconography. But because of the placement of his hand on Obama's wrist (rather than palm), because of the substantial height differential and because Obama didn't reciprocate, Castro ended up holding aloft a limp Obama hand. Interpretations greatly differed as to who came out looking better. Did it seem like Obama was a puppet and the communist a puppeteer? Or was it in fact a stroke of genius? For the *Guardian*,

> It is a move that may be taught to aspiring diplomats for decades to come. Had he tried to wriggle free, the abiding image of the first trip by a US president in 88 years would have been one of continued political struggle. Had he simply left a straight arm aloft, Obama would have gifted the Cubans the photo opportunity of the century: a US president vindicating the revolution with a socialist salute.[10]

In international diplomacy, the optics of the handshake are everything – but you can only work with what you've got.

The assassination of a president by way of a handshake

The American President William McKinley was known for the 'McKinley grip', an incredibly efficient handshake which reportedly allowed him to shake fifty hands a minute on the campaign trail. The problem with this type of handshake (or indeed any politician's handshake) is the trade-off between the special connection with people derived from hand-to-hand contact and the security problems that come with proximity to that same group of people. In fact, fears of assassination attempts against McKinley had already led to efforts to get him to cancel certain hand-shaking events and add more people to his security detail. The president resisted; it remained a constant tug of war until, on 6 September 1901, he visited the World Fair in Buffalo, New York, where he was killed by Leon Czolgosz. Czolgosz used the pretence of the handshake to get close to him – which is sadly ironic, given that the president considered shaking hands with the public to be his favourite part of the job.

Czolgosz had got close to the podium where the president was speaking the day before and had debated shooting him then, but was unsure that it would be a direct hit. Instead, he joined a crowd of would-be hand-shakers. People were supposed to approach the president with hands that were empty and open, but when, at 4.07 p.m., Czolgosz approached with his right hand wrapped in a handkerchief, McKinley thought he was injured and reached for his assassin's left hand. Czolgosz shot him twice.

As we've seen, there is a common belief (which I do not share) that the handshake is simply a sign of not having a weapon, a visual demonstration of good intentions. But, as McKinley's death demonstrates, it also provides the opportunity to get close enough to inflict harm – a reminder that our desire for reciprocal connection makes us vulnerable too.

7

Demise: Is This the End of the Handshake?

It's the end of the world as we know it

As the COVID-19 pandemic got under way, I saw headlines screaming that our lives would never be the same again. Friends and colleagues whom I respect were acting as if it was the end of civilisation. New York was pronounced 'dead' (to the fury of Jerry Seinfeld). It started feeling like hysteria.

The eminent Professor Francois Balloux, of my own institution, University College London, rightfully decried headlines like 'There is no getting "back to normal", experts say. The sooner we accept that, the better.'[1] Firstly, because it's very poor public-health messaging: tell people that all is lost and they're probably not going to bother to social-distance around Grandma. And secondly, because this isn't the first deadly pandemic! In AD 541–2, 25–100 million people died during the Plague of Justinian, which was followed by the many other iterations of the plague, including the Black Death. Within living memory (just), we had the Spanish flu of 1918 in which 500 million people died worldwide. More recently we had SARS, HIV, the cholera pandemic of 1961–75 and the 2009–10 swine flu pandemic. They were agonising experiences, tragedies, some of epic proportions, but in every case 'civilisation' and 'life as we know it' stuck around; both, it seems, are pretty damn resilient. Perhaps a by-product of thankfully living in a stable, industrialised country is that we have become out of touch with the instability and danger in which others live around the globe. I work in politically unstable, hostile and disputed territories, and I've seen people, including my family, live in war zones and not declare that it is the end of civilisation. Good lord, even the Nazis, who *lost* a whole world war, have recently been marching in Charlottesville, incurring the anti-wrath of the then occupant of the White House. My nan, a Scouser, keeps declaring that she's lived through 'the war', as if she is trying to give us all some perspective.

Huge, singular events rarely create complete systemic overhauls in behaviour – at best they shift the needle along a trajectory. HIV, for example, was significant in changing attitudes to safe sex, but it wasn't the only thing; other sexually transmitted diseases and fear of pregnancy also played a role. Additionally, clearly not everyone has changed their views on safe sex! What we should be asking is how COVID-19 might change our behaviour, and will it last? From the beginning of the pandemic, public-health messaging focused on hands as a source of infection; on washing them, and advising against handshakes entirely. The handshake had fallen abruptly out of favour. Suddenly the media were filled with stories about politicians' hapless attempts to deal with the new reality; in March 2020 Angela Merkel was caught on camera first extending a hand to Interior Minister Horst Seehofer, who anxiously waved it away, and then commending him for following the rules.[2] In the same month the Dutch prime minister, fresh from the announcement of a national no-shake policy, turned around and immediately shook hands with a health official. 'Oh, sorry!' he said. 'We can't do that any more. Sorry, sorry.'[3]

As the handshake faded away, the depth with which it was ingrained in our societies was revealed. For some this was a matter of social awkwardness: hands sheepishly retracted, nervous laughter as people tried this new elbow-bump thing, as if it was the new TikTok dance craze. Sometimes the results were more far-reaching: pity the applicants for Danish citizenship who were left in limbo because the naturalisation ceremony legally required a handshake.[4] As our leaders experimented with hands on hearts, elbow bumps and namastes, in some quarters the handshake assumed a symbolic role; avoiding it showed you were responsible and taking things seriously, while continuing to press the flesh signalled a devil-may-care, business-as-usual attitude that began to ring hollow as the death toll climbed. Donald Trump, on record as describing the handshake as 'barbaric' ('shaking hands, you catch colds, you catch the flu, you catch it, you catch all sorts of things. Who knows what you don't catch?')[5] , suddenly became a diehard advocate. As the journalist Megan Garber put it, these were handshakes as 'empty assurances: signals that the pandemic was not as dire as the experts were warning it was. The leaders' particular definition of liberty would include the freedom to shake hands – even when the hands themselves could pose risks to other people.'[6]

If the only people arguing for your existence are the ones who are seemingly happy to endanger others just to make a political statement or to give false reassurances, then you might think you have a problem. But accounts of the death of the handshake – however sensible avoiding it is as a temporary measure is – run counter to the lessons of history, for 2020 was far from the first time that its demise was declared. Not by a long shot.

Exit the handshake

The Greek historian Thucydides, a survivor of the Plague of Athens (430–427 BC) which killed a third of the inhabitants of the city, provides the only eyewitness account of the epidemic. In *The History of the Peloponnesian War* he writes about how social norms broke down as the disease tightened its grip on the population: 'as the disaster passed all bounds, men, not knowing what was to become of them, became utterly careless of everything, whether sacred or profane. All the burial rites before in use were entirely upset, and they buried the bodies as best they could.'[7] A bleak picture, but not an unfamiliar one, as anyone who saw the depressing satellite images of mass graves dug in Iran or Yemen during the first months of the COVID-19 pandemic could testify.[8]

In fact, there is very little about the COVID-19 pandemic that is unique and original in terms of public-health responses. Quarantine, isolation, social distancing, schools, institutions and government buildings being closed, people fleeing infested cities, fear of strangers or outsiders – these reactions are historically seen time and again. Even mask-wearing isn't new: during the 1918 flu pandemic, the *Republic* newspaper described New York as 'a city of masked faces, a city as grotesque as a masked carnival'.[9] And on the other side of the world, in Sydney, 'it was noted that while face masks were compulsory, there were "many fewer" cases of influenza'.[10] There was often a recognition that touch might be connected to the transmission of disease, and the regulation of physical contact is a recurring theme – either voluntarily or by the state. What we would recognise as rational and effective responses to disease anticipated the germ theory which would, hundreds of years later, back them up: a decree to ban the kiss was issued by the Roman Emperor Tiberius (r. AD 14–37), after mentagra, a disfiguring fungoid disease, began working its way through the Roman nobility. It usually started at the chin, and kissing was thought to be behind its spread.[11]

In 1439 the English Parliament had not met for over a year because of the bubonic plague, but financial and military pressures were building up. An anxious-sounding Commons petitioned the teenaged (and childless) Henry VI to allow them not to perform the kiss of homage and instead accept letters, in order to protect him from contagion. This was a big deal, as it was the first ceremonial kiss performed by the lieges of the king to him as an adult:[12]

> We, your poor true liege people, considering and desiring the health and welfare of your most noble person above all earthly things ... beseech your most noble grace, in conserving of your most noble person ... in avoiding any such infection to fall on you, God forbid ... that each of your lieges in the doing of their said homage may omit the said kissing of you and be excused thereof at your will.[13]

In another familiar twist a few decades later, during another outbreak of plague in 1518, the inhabitants of

Windsor instituted strict quarantine and social-distancing regulations:

> Any castle inhabitant who became infected was to be quarantined immediately and the door of the house shut up, limiting access. Access into and out of quarantined houses was also strictly limited. One person only was permitted to leave the house, to fetch food, drink and other necessities for the other quarantined individuals. He was required to carry a four-foot-long white rod upright while out of quarantine, so that other members of the castle community could maintain their distance and avoid the possibility of infection.[14]

The ordinance – basically, a four-foot pole of shame – also applied to London. In addition, an eight-foot pole was stuck to the side of the quarantined house, with a 'wisp of hay or straw on the end' to warn passers-by and allow them to avoid infection.

This understanding of the dangers of proximity and touch in terms of contagion sometimes directly involved the handshake. In 1793, a devastating yellow-fever epidemic hit the city of Philadelphia, then capital of the USA. The Irish American publisher and economist Matthew Carey, who wrote widely about the epidemic and its impact on the city and the government, estimated that out of 50,000 Philadelphians, 17,000 left the city and 4,000 died (though it may have been as many as 5,000). Most of the wealthy left over the summer, and President George Washington and his family followed on 10 September, as did almost everyone from the city, state and national governments.[15] Carey writes of 'frightful scenes', and that 'when people summoned up resolution to walk abroad, and take the air, the sick-cart conveying patients to the hospital, or the hearse carrying the dead to the grave, which were traveling almost the whole day, soon damped their spirits, and plunged them again into despondency'.[16] And he adds that 'the old custom of shaking hands fell in such general disuse, that many shrunk back with affright at even the offer of a hand'.[17] (Sounds familiar, right?) This was one of the worst epidemics that the USA – still a relatively young nation which had only adopted the Declaration of Independence in 1776 – had experienced, affecting the seat of power and the movers and shakers of the new republic.[18] The conditions were right to change the course of the handshake's future in the USA. It is strange, then, that this epidemic was no more than a temporary setback to the handshake.

With deeper understanding of how contagion spread came more direct criticism of the handshake. But first I want to share a sad coda to the story of hand hygiene and disease. Ignaz Philipp Semmelweis was a Hungarian physician, scientist and pioneer of antiseptic procedures; when working in a hospital in Vienna, he noticed that newborns delivered by doctors were dying of puerperal fever at a higher rate than those who were born with the assistance of midwives. He concluded that doctors were picking the infection up from the autopsies they also performed and then transferring it to the babies. In 1847, he suggested that washing one's hands with a chlorinated lime solution could save lives. He was ridiculed by colleagues, and the ensuing controversy ended with his committal to an asylum, where he died two weeks later, after a beating from the asylum guards, in a tragically ironic manner – from a gangrenous wound on his hand, 'the very disease that he had struggled so hard to prevent'.[19]

Semmelweis's theory would later be proved accurate by the work of Louis Pasteur and Joseph Lister, amongst others. A basic understanding of germ theory appears to have influenced the establishment of an anti-handshake society in Baku (in modern-day Azerbaijan, then part of Russia) which was set up because of fears of cholera in 1894 and reported with some amusement in the Western press. 'Members pay six roubles a year, and wear a button as a sign of membership. They are fined three roubles for each handshake … The ridiculous lengths to which fear of contagion will lead one is illustrated in the city of Baku,' said the *Corpuscle*,[20] a publication associated with Rush Medical College in Chicago, while *The Lancet*, at its cattiest, snarked: 'It is not often that the worship of scientific truth exhibits itself in a form so literal and so ostentatious. It is in this case the more remarkable since among the Russian people sanitary measures have hitherto been distinguished by their virtual abeyance.'[21] This take, from the world's most famous medical journal, hasn't aged well, and it's hard to deny that the eccentric Baku club were on to something. Though I don't see many in the COVID-19 economic climate volunteering for the handshake equivalent of a swear jar.

By the time the Spanish flu pandemic swept the globe in 1918, the link between contagion and hand-shaking was much more widely accepted. In a 'Hands. Face. Space.' piece of messaging, the residents of Milwaukee were urged by their Health Department to avoid 'public places and crowded streets' and community sing-songs, since 'unfortunately many have rather a moist way of singing'. They were also urged to 'get out of the habit of bringing the hands to the mouth', and informed that 'the handshake as a form of salutation should be abandoned'.[22] In 1919, Dr H. W. Hill, in an on-the-nose opinion piece titled 'Danger in handshake is seen by physician', wrote: 'no one should be so foolhardy as to refuse to take every precaution against [the epidemic]. The first precaution we should like to see enforced is this – universal ban on the handshake.'[23] Prescott, Arizona, took it to its logical conclusion and made it illegal to shake hands.

As I surveyed the medical literature, it was clear that a timeline of handshake-dissent amongst medical profess- sionals was developing – beginning perhaps unsurprisingly around the time of the Spanish flu. As the twentieth century wore on, suspicion of the handshake became firmly embed- ded in the medical zeitgeist, and alternatives began to be suggested. In 1926 the *Ohio Health News* announced, perhaps a tad melodramatically, that 'the honest, hearty handshake may and frequently does transfer just as many pathogenic bacteria as though a deadly enemy were conceal- ing his mortal designs in such a greeting', before going on to advocate the Chinese custom of 'shaking one's own hand': 'We make a lot of fun of China, but often may profit by her ancient wisdom if we but would. At least, your own germs will stay at home if you shake your own hand.'[24] In 1929, a nurse, Leila Given, also suggested the Chinese method, while lamenting the disappearance of 'finger-tipping and the high hand-shake'. But even amongst these hopeful suggestions of more hygienic alternatives, there is a note of realism: both these authors doubt whether the handshake will ever fall out of use.

Ninety years later, health-care professionals are still

arguing against it: Dr Ian McCurdie, the British Olympic Association's head doctor, made international headlines in 2012 when he suggested that British athletes might be wise to avoid shaking hands with their competitors and visiting dignitaries during the London Olympic Games in order to avoid illness.[25] After a cholera outbreak in Zimbabwe in 2018, the Health and Child Care Minister Dr David Parirenyatwa urged people to not shake hands at funerals, suggesting a fist bump or elbow bump if absolutely necessary.[26] And in 2014, at the height of the Ebola epidemic in Liberia, many inhabitants in Ebola-infected regions abandoned their distinctive Liberian finger snap, a kind of handshake which involves snapping each other's fingers as the hands withdraw, it being a point of pride to produce the loudest noise.

All of these incidents point to the sheer resilience of the handshake. You'll have noticed that if it died out in Philadelphia in the eighteenth century, it was still around to get banned in Arizona in 1918, and again for Anthony Fauci to get in on the act over a hundred years later. Mentagra, the chin-based fungal infection of Imperial Rome, certainly sounds like it's worth avoiding, and yet we still kiss each other in the twenty-first century (the Italians certainly do). In Liberia, the handshake started returning (along with other traditional greeting customs) when a vaccine for Ebola was rolled out. Under pressure our behaviour alters, but not in lasting ways. It appears that only the immediate fear of death or serious illness is enough to suppress our need to shake hands – and even then it is just temporary.

Get your filthy paws off me

Even if you take into account humans' tendency to make some poor decisions regarding their personal safety, the resilience of the handshake is somewhat surprising given that the anti-handshake lobby is, er, absolutely right in this regard. Our hands are covered in bacteria, and the handshake is a particularly good way of passing them on from one person to another. Hands are simply awesome vessels for the transfer of material; the appendage that sends chemosignals between people, aiding communication, turns out to be equally effective at conveying bacteria and viruses.

The scientific literature proving that our hands have bacteria and viruses on them is too extensive to summarise, but I'll provide an overview. Our skin microbiome is made up of billions of bacteria – 'up to 1×10^7 bacteria per cm^2' according to one scientific overview[27] – most of which are harmless or even beneficial to us, even at these mind-boggling levels. But as well as the ones we carry with us, there are the ones we pick up from touching surfaces, objects, other people and ourselves, meaning that our hands, the vectors by which we interact with the world, are particularly abundant environments: most people harbour more than 150 bacterial species on the palms of their hands, some even viruses and fungi.[28]

There's plenty of evidence that bacteria and viruses survive on hands for a while after the original contact: rhinoviruses, which cause the common cold, are particularly resilient, with 50 per cent–100 per cent of the original transfer detectable on hands after three hours. The influenza virus isn't so hardy, but studies have found it lingering on hands in a viable form for between thirty minutes and an hour.[29] Transfer to other hands or surfaces seems to be particularly likely if you've got a runny nose: a 1947 study found the 'hands of nasal carriers of hemolytic streptococci [a common bacteria which causes, amongst other things, pneumonia] and of individuals who shook hands with these carriers showed that several hundred to as many as 49,900 of these pathogens could be transferred by ordinary hand-shakes. The greatest numbers were transferred by carriers who had just blown their noses into sterile handkerchiefs.' Similarly, there appears to be greater transfer of bacteria in the presence of 'sputum', a mixture of mucus and saliva, which is expelled, for example, by coughing into your hand.[30]

All of this makes it relatively unsurprising that if you want to avoid getting ill you should a) wash your hands (probably with soap and hot water rather than alcohol gel) and b) not touch someone else's hands. But in particular, perhaps, avoid the handshake: another study found that bacterial transfer was reduced by 50 per cent with a 'high-five' hand slap compared to a handshake, and by 80 per cent to 90 per cent with a fist bump. A strong handshake led to greater bacterial transfer.[31] (It should be noted that the study only covered bacterial transfer, and not viruses – although it seems reasonable to assume that the same effect would be noticeable.) The data on fist bumps as a more hygienic alter-native is controversial,[32] although a further study (looking at MRSA) found that, while a fist bump wasn't significantly better than a handshake, 'transfer was significantly reduced with a modified fist bump that reduced the area of contact to a single knuckle and when patient hand hygiene was per-formed before a handshake'.[33] You have to wonder whether touching a single knuckle can really be called a 'modified fist bump'; it's such a shadow of itself it hardly seems worth the effort.

Interestingly, most of the suggestions for handshake avoidance still involve touch and getting close to people – doctors working in 'handshake-free zones' in hospitals have tried to create the same sense of intimacy and trust fostered by the handshake by touching a shoulder, or with the elbow bump. In some respects the most serious challenger to the handshake, the elbow bump was first introduced internationally by the WHO during an epidemic of avian flu in 2006 (having previously been used to help fight Ebola). Its public debut was made in the *New York Times*: 'To the pantheon of social arbiters who came up with the firm handshake, the formal bow and the air kiss, get ready to add a new fashion god: the World Health Organization, chief advocate of the "elbow bump".'[34] Barack Obama was an early adopter.

The appeal of the elbow bump is presumably, as the *New York Times* article puts it, due to the fact that 'only a contortionist can sneeze on his elbow' – like the fist bump, it maintains the element of all-important physical contact while managing the risk. But people just don't seem to like these bumps as much; even doctors who had a strong motivation to manage the spread of infection worried about seeming 'rude' when they rejected an offered handshake, and were concerned that it would make it harder to connect with patients.[35] And while some patients appeared to accept the avoidance of the handshake on health grounds, they didn't like the alternatives, with respondents to one survey finding the fist bump too easy to mistake for 'an aggressive act', before adding that it was a 'stupid idea. Wash your hands.'[36]

There are some grounds for this view – that the problem is less the handshake than the poor hygiene of the hand-shaker. After all, if you're still using your dirty paws to open doors and so on, avoiding handshakes isn't going to protect society. Sadly, the bad news is that we're even worse at washing our hands than we are at stopping shaking hands. In 2017, a global study found that only about 19 per cent of people wash their hands after faecal contact.[37] There are variations: it appears that women are significantly better at hand-washing compliance than men, for example, and of course access to clean water and soap varies across the world.[38] But, generally, we suck at this, and it's pretty obvious why you should wash your hands when you've been to the loo; people often wonder if *that study* of urine on peanuts in pubs is true or some urban legend. It is actually worse than people think: when journalists from the *Evening Standard* tested snacks in London pubs they could only declare of some of them that 'This sample was free of faecal contamination'.[39] So ... poo on peanuts. This reminds me of the time my friend ran out of a toilet cubicle and went straight for the door. When I protested, 'Dude, wash your hands,' she looked at me and said it was 'just wee'. Oh, well, if it's just urine, forgive me. As you were. She might be part of the problem.

So, does COVID-19 spell the end of the handshake? To my mind, as long as it's the only large-scale deadly pandemic in a given time period – the only 'once-in-a-century pandemic' – then the evidence is pretty clear: it's not a question of whether the handshake will return, but when. It might be dirty, unhealthy and even banned – but once the immediate pressure is off, the handshake will return. It always does. The constant resurrection of the darn thing, its sheer bloody resilience, is a testament to its significance to us, its power and universality as a gesture and its deep intertwining with our biology.

Epilogue

So, what next for the handshake? For a moment there, people certainly thought the handshake was teetering on the brink of disaster, and this most positive and useful of gestures still has its detractors (here's looking at you, Dr Fauci, and your wistful hope that perhaps we'll never shake hands again). But as I write this, in the midst of a London lockdown and with social-distancing protocols still firmly in place across the globe, I don't think we're witnessing the death of the handshake: I think what we're seeing is, at most, a disruption.

Time and again – from Philadelphia in 1793 to Baku in 1894 – we've seen the handshake and other haptic greetings disappear as a result of disease, epidemics and pandemics. And yet it's never gone for good: time and time and time again we see it rise from the dead. Of course, some have speculated that we are about to enter an 'Age of Pandemics', during which our traditions of touch-based greeting might fade away under sustained, repeated onslaughts. I don't really see the evidence for that – we were, after all, overdue a truly deadly pandemic, given that it had been over a century since the Spanish flu – but *if* we are looking at an Age of Pandemics it is certainly true that humans can alter deeply rooted behaviour. Societies are capable of massive cultural changes that continue shifting along a trajectory – in response to multiple events, creating an additive effect, such as women's liberation and the way in which the women's suffrage movement blossomed into the radical shift that occurred during the Second World War when women entered the workforce en masse.

Something that might make a difference would be a genuine challenger: a gesture and greeting which provided the same benefits as the handshake, but without the risk of, er, catching a deadly disease. So, in the interests of giving them a fair hearing, I have rounded up the possible alternatives to the handshake; in lieu of the handshake I give you:

Greeting	Description	Positive	Negative
The fist bump	We all know the fist bump. Its most famous proponent is perhaps Barack Obama. His fist bump with Michelle at the 2008 Democratic convention when he won the nomination went national and then became a staple of his.	Decreased chance of contagion. Upon seeing Obama do it, a Fox News anchor declared that it could be a seen as a 'terrorist fist jab'. So really … it's also a litmus test for idiots.	For some years pushed by some medical professionals as a less haptic (and thus less unsanitary) handshake, the fist bump is still too haptic for COVID-19.

Greeting	Description	Positive	Negative
The elbow bump	Why should two people introduce their sweaty palms when they can introduce their funny bones?	It has the most positive PR of all the handshake alternatives – it has the whiff of a handshake, but upon closer inspection it isn't. It is basically a knock-off designer handbag: you quickly realise it is not the real thing, but it is probably better for you.	There aren't as many touch receptors in our elbows, which is probably why we weren't elbow-bumping in the Palaeolithic Age. Additionally, you actually have to get closer to each other to perform this than a handshake! It is fascinating that the WHO gold-standard substitute for the handshake now officially breaks social-distancing rules. Also, let's be honest, it is like being told you are getting a Hemsworth brother and then being sent Luke. (I mean, it's fine … but you thought you were getting Chris or Liam.)

The Handshake

Greeting	Description	Positive	Negative
The Wuhan shake	Tapping a foot against your partner's, or both feet in close succession.	Creates a bit more distance than the elbow bump and is quite fun to do.	In the Arab world anything to do with feet is a real sign of disrespect – so it's not going to work for everybody. Also, it still isn't going to maintain a two-metre distance, unless Peter Crouch and Stephen Merchant stumble upon each other.
The Wakanda hand-shake	Taken from the film *Black Panther*. Fists clenched, arms crossed over the chest. Apparently, the salute was partly inspired by American Sign Language for hug or love.	It comes from a different (better) universe than our own, so it is aspirational. Plus … it's cool.	I'm struggling to see some of the people in the City or Wall Street adopting this one.
The Regency bow or curtsey	You can find a how-to guide in any Jane Austen adaptation.	Compliant with social-distancing rules … *and* feels like 'dressing up'!	Highly gendered, harks back to a deeply inegalitarian era. The cosplay way of saying 'we've had enough of our dalliance with equality!'

Greeting	Description	Positive	Negative
The top hat tip	For those of us who went through a fedora-wearing hipster phase, and now don't know what to do with our accessories.	I have hats.	You need a (top) hat. At best you'll seem mildly eccentric, at worst it's a gateway drug to using words like 'methinks' and 'spiffing' in general conversation.
The Japanese bow	Performed from the waist.	I think it is fair to say that if the Japanese were known for their smugness, which they aren't, they would be exhibiting a lot of it right now. It is incredibly COVID-era friendly, as are so many of the Far East's no-touch greetings.	Maybe too closely associated with Japanese culture to be adopted globally – and this won't translate well to the Muslim world, where it might be seen as prostration.
Black Power salute	Contains a powerful message of Black Power, excellence and solidarity. For non-Black people, note that it's about solidarity with Black people and that its meaning shouldn't be diluted: perfect for a Black Lives Matter protest.	It's wonderful; the Black Power salute at the 1968 Olympics still gives me chills.	Probably don't do this in Tesco.

Greeting	Description	Positive	Negative
The selfie	Shaking hands with yourself, recommended by Stephen Colbert (and slightly similar to the traditional Chinese greeting).	It's like faking a handshake, even down to the choreography. Also, it keeps you in practice!	Thanks to lockdown, some might have had enough of touching themselves.
The shaka sign	Hand in a fist but with thumb and pinkie extended. Then shake it.	It is associated with Hawaiian and surfer culture – there are no literal translations, but it means everything from hang loose to friendship. It has a 'vibe', and that vibe is a positive and sunny one.	Doesn't seem quite at home in rainy, cloudy London or Birmingham.
Jazz hands	Hands splayed and held next to your chest, then waggle energetically.	To quote the satirical magazine *Broadway Beat*, 'If we have any hope of saving the world from this crippling disease, by God, it is with sassy, interpretative movement.'	Hard to summon up the energy to do this one properly if you're not in the mood.

Of course, if this *really* were a competition to find a challenger to the handshake, it would be hard to pick a winner. Not because there isn't much exceptional talent in the game, but because nothing compares to last year's winner, who also won every annual competition for the last 7 million years. No wonder nothing matches up.

The handshake has its disadvantages: it's unsanitary and sometimes freighted with expectation and pointless rules. Getting it wrong can feel embarrassing. But if COVID-19 has taught us anything, it's that touch really matters – and our impulse to do it likely comes from deep within our DNA. As a basic unit of touch, nothing works as well as the handshake: it allows us to transmit chemosignals, build trust, gesture quickly and universally, send positive signals of agreement, unity and acceptance. The cultural identity of the handshake whereby it represents equality and respect is one to celebrate, too, as is its presence across the world in diverse and specialised forms. In all its manifestations – from finger-snapping to its value in business, its historical significance and use by chimps – we should celebrate it for the versatile, positive, helpful gesture it is. Human history would look very different without it.

To quote one of my comedy heroes, Stephen Colbert, discussing the possible death of the handshake with another comedy titan, Jerry Seinfeld: when we are let loose on the vaccine, 'there is going to be a great rubbing of parts'. Anything as deeply entrenched in our culture, biology and probably DNA as the handshake is, quite frankly, going nowhere. That doesn't mean it won't be a difficult journey; I remember how my first hugs and handshakes with men were surreal, existing somewhere between nerve-wracking and hyper-awareness of what felt like every touch receptor in my hand. I suspect that something slightly similar is in store for you, my friends; those first few handshakes you embark on post COVID-19 will be memorable sensory experiences. But you will be ecstatic about them. I am writing this at Christmas 2020, in London, in Tier 4. It is about eight months since I have shaken hands with anyone. For now, this makes sense – it is not the time for handshakes – but when this crisis is over, I'm going to be the weirdo not just shaking strangers' hands but holding their hands tightly for the entire meeting. Some of us waited a long time to shake hands, and spent a long time looking for alternatives. And I'm telling you: nothing lives up to the handshake.

Acknowledgements

Towards the end of 2020, I had a three-week period that can only be described as a scheduling nightmare: I was supposed to be delivering this book, I had two TV series going out ... and then I almost died after a trip to the dentist. I wish I knew how to express my gratitude to all who work at University College London Hospital, especially Mr Adrian Farrow and his colleagues. I will never forget what you did – nor will I forget your faces when I tried negotiating a way for you to discharge me before emergency surgery if I promised to come back after my deadlines. Bless you, our NHS and the other patients on my ward and their caring, watchful eyes.

If this book is terrible, please blame my old dentist. If it is any good, then it is my editor's fault: after I got ill Cecily Gayford went truly above and beyond to get it across the finishing line. I can't thank her enough. I am also hugely grateful to the team at Profile Books: Graeme Hall, Shona Abhyankar and my copy-editor Linden Lawson, who all worked incredibly hard to make the book happen on a short, and then even shorter, schedule.

As the first lockdown started, I was quickly, and rightly, being benched from my TV projects and expeditions across

Somaliland, Iraq and all over the place. I owe a debt of gratitude to my agents: my literary agent, Julian Alexander, who dreamt up the idea of a book on the handshake, and my TV agent, Sophie Laurimore, who suggested that they talk to me about it. What a remarkably well-suited 'lockdown project'. Thanks also to my publicist, Anna Penney, who, along with my agency, did all kinds of heavy lifting and picked up a lot of slack once I got ill.

Dan Stone is my literary fairy godfather and Jessica Cramp my writing buddy and rock: without them I would never have motivated myself to write a book. Liz Farebrother provided much help and research insights, as did Dr Jo Msindai, Dr Peggy Brown, Anna Westland and Paul Urenda. This book would of course not have been possible without the research and conclusions of hundreds of researchers whose sweat, toil and sometimes life's work had me in awe and helped me build an argument.

My housemate Rachael Sykes was my lockdown partner in crime and her enthusiasm for this book was much needed when mine would wane. Brigitte Salomon opened up her chalet in the Swiss Alps for me when I needed a change of scenery between lockdowns and a writing retreat; thank you for your friendship, and thank you to Alison Langley for introducing me to that valley. I'm so glad to have been writing my first book at the same time that Ellie Taylor was writing hers. She is a dear, supportive friend … and on a regular basis demonstrates that whatever I can do, she can do with a toddler in tow.

Jane Marriott, Ash Javed, Dr Rachel Souhami, Dr Kathleen Bryson, Madeleine Foote, Tom Dale, Carlos Suarez, Susie Steed, Louisa Loveluck, Melissa Llewelyn-Davies,

Acknowledgements

Rosa and Richard Curling, Wesley Della Volla and Ben Romberg provided incredible amounts of help, support and encouragement, sometimes in conjunction with flowers and brownies. Thanks to all my friends, colleagues and strangers online for your kind words and well wishes.

Finally, to my nan, my cousins Baraa Shiban and Najah Almujahid, Carla Stephan, my sister-in-law Duaa Altholaya, my dear parents and 'my everything' siblings Assad, Abubakr and Aaya and of course my big sister Asma, who is our mother hen – I love you and I can't wait to hug you all again. It's been too long and too painful.

Notes

Introduction

1. Bryan Lufkin, 'Will Covid-19 end the handshake?', BBC, 14 April 2020, https://www.bbc.com/worklife/article/20200413-coronavirus-will-covid-19-end-the-handshake

2. Amy Gunia, '"I don't think we should ever shake hands again." Dr Fauci says Coronavirus should change some behaviors for good', *Time*, 9 April 2020, https://time.com/5818134/anthony-fauci-never-shake-hands-coronavirus/

3. Many thanks to my editor, Cecily Gayford, for coining the phrase 'unit of touch'.

4. 'Daily question', YouGov, 16 March 2020, accessed 7 January 2021, https://yougov.co.uk/topics/health/survey-results/daily/2020/03/16/abde6/3

5. For non-Brits, Dominic Cummings was Boris Johnson's most senior advisor (they later became enemies), but during the first national lockdown, having very recently caught Covid-19, Cummings was seen at Barnard Castle. In a press conference he claimed his trip was to test his eyesight before

embarking on a 253-mile journey back home to London.

1. Origin Story: Where Does the Handshake Come From?

1. The 1928 Sugar Expedition in New Guinea by the US Department of Agriculture was led by E. W. Brandes. For the image see p. 53 and figure 5 of Joshua Bell, 'Sugar plant hunting by airplane in New Guinea', *Journal of Pacific History* 45 (3 June 2010), pp. 37–56, https://doi.org/10.1080/00223344.2010. 484166. Additional information: the Smithsonian archive, https://sova.si.edu/record/NAA.PhotoLot.91– 8?s=0&n=10&t=A&q=Sugarcane&i=1. The sixty-four-minute film can be found in the Smithsonian Institution's Human Studies Film Archives, Suitland, MD, and is a silent 35mm black-and-white film called *Sugar plant hunting by airplane in New Guinea*. Brandes wrote a book titled *Into Primeval Papua by Seaplane: Seeking Disease-Resisting Sugar Cane Neolithic Man Found in Unmapped Nooks of Sorcery & Cannibalism* (Washington: National Geographic, 1929).

2. 'Sir David Attenborough greets a group of cannibals', Snotr, accessed 7 January 2021, https://www. snotr.com/video/11354/Sir_David_Attenborough_ greets_a_group_of_cannibals. Also see Richard Luke, 'David Attenborough', *Esquire Middle East*, 24 April 2014, accessed 7 January 2021, https:// www.esquireme.com/culture/what-ive-learned/

what-ive-learned-david-attenborough. It is not clear what language Attenborough uses to communicate, but while describing it he tells it as if they speak 'pidgin' English. This seems unlikely given the colonial history and the remoteness of the tribes; it was also, and still is, common amongst some to recount stories that involve tribes as if their language is 'pidgin' English, even when a translator is actually the means of communication.

3. Irenäus Eibl-Eibesfeldt, *Love and Hate: The Natural History of Behavior Patterns* (New York: Aldine De Gruyter, 1996).

4. From here on, 'chimps' in the text refers to both common chimpanzees and bonobos.

5. Many thanks to Dr Cat Hobaiter at the University of St Andrews for this research and for sharing her findings with me even though not all of them had been published at the time of writing this book.

6. Joyce Poole, 'Visual communication', *Elephant Voices*, accessed 7 January 2021, https://www.elephantvoices. org/elephant-communication/visual-communication. html

7. Christine Dell'Amore, 'Venomous primate discovered in Borneo', *National Geographic*, 15 December 2012, accessed 7 January 2021, https:// www.nationalgeographic.com/news/2012/12/ venomous-primate-discovered-in-borneo/

8. Michio Nakamura, 'Grooming-hand-clasp in Mahale M Group chimpanzees', in Christophe Boesch et al. (eds), *Behavioural Diversity in Chimpanzees and*

Bonobos (Cambridge: Cambridge University Press, 2002), pp. 71–89.

9. Frans de Waal, *The Bonobo and the Atheist* (New York: W. W. Norton & Company, 2013).

10. Eibl-Eibesfeldt, *Love and Hate*.

11. Rob Dunn, 'Sick people smell bad: Why dogs sniff dogs, humans sniff humans, and dogs sometimes sniff humans', *Scientific American*, 15 January 2015, accessed 8 January 2021, https://blogs. scientificamerican.com/guest-blog/sick-people-smell-bad-why-dogs-sniff-dogs-humans-sniff-humans-and-dogs-sometimes-sniff-humans/

12. Paula Jendrny et al., 'Scent dog identification of samples from COVID-19 patients – a pilot study', *BMC Infect Dis* 20, 536 (2020), https://doi. org/10.1186/s12879-020-05281-3

13. Biagio D'Aniello et al., 'Interspecies transmission of emotional information via chemosignals: From humans to dogs (*Canis lupus familiaris*)', *Anim Cogn* 21, pp. 67–78 (2018), https://doi.org/10.1007/ s10071-017-1139-x

14. Aras Petrulis, 'Chemosignals, hormones and mammalian reproduction', *Hormones and Behavior* 63, 5 (2013), pp. 723–41, doi:10.1016/j. yhbeh.2013.03.011

15. D. Chen and J. Haviland-Jones, 'Human olfactory communication of emotion', *Perceptual and Motor Skills* 91, 3, Pt 1 (2000), pp. 771–81, doi:10.2466/pms.2000.91.3.771; Jasper de Groot et al., 'Chemosignals communicate human emotions', *Psychological Science* 23, 11 (2012),

pp. 1417–24, accessed 8 January 2021, http://www.jstor.org/stable/23484546; Jasper de Groot et al., 'A sniff of happiness', *Psychological Science* 26, 6 (June 2015), pp. 684–700, https://doi.org/10.1177/0956797614566318

16. Chen and Haviland-Jones, 'Human olfactory communication of emotion'.

17. Shani Gelstein, 'Human tears contain a chemosignal', *Science* 331, 6014 (14 January 2011), pp. 226–30, doi: https://science.sciencemag.org/content/331/6014/226

18. Idan Frumin, 'A social chemosignaling function for human handshaking', *ELife* 4 (3 March 2015), E05154, https://elifesciences.org/articles/05154; Gün Semin and Ana R. Farias, 'Social chemosignaling: The scent of a handshake', *ELife* 4 (3 March 2015), E06758, doi: https://elifesciences.org/articles/06758

19. Ashley Fetters, 'The exceptional cruelty of a no-hugging policy', *The Atlantic*, 20 June 2018, accessed 8 January 2021, https://www.theatlantic.com/family/archive/2018/06/family-separation-no-hugging-policy/563294/

20. There is a direct correlation between higher oxytocin levels in a mother in the first trimester of pregnancy and an increase in mother–child bonding behaviours like singing or bathing the child. Dads who received a nasal squirt of oxytocin could also be shown to increase their father–child bonding behaviours.

21. Carsten de Dreu et al., 'Oxytocin promotes human ethnocentrism', *PNAS* 108, 4 (25 January 2011), pp. 1262–6, https://doi.org/10.1073/pnas.1015316108

22. Paul Zak, 'The power of a handshake: How touch

sustains personal and business relationships',
HuffPost, 30 October 2008, accessed 8 January 2021,
https://www.huffpost.com/entry/the-power-of-a-hands
hake_b_129441?guccounter=1; Paul Zak, 'Handshake
or hug? Why we touch', *Psychology Today*, 5 October
2008, accessed 8 January 2021, https://www.
psychologytoday.com/us/blog/the-moral-
molecule/200810/handshake-or-hug-why-we-touch

23. Michael Lynn, 'Increasing servers' tips: What
    managers can do and why they should do it', Cornell
    University, School of Hospitality Administration site
    (2005), accessed 8 January 2021, http://scholarship.sha.
    cornell.edu/articles/98

24. Irenäus Eibl-Eibesfeldt, 'The expressive behaviour
    of the deaf-and-blind-born', in M. von Cranach
    and I. Vine (eds), *Social Communication and
    Movement* (London: Academic, 1973), pp. 163–94.

25. Colleen Walsh, 'Wither the handshake? Harvard
    experts weigh in on the origin and fate of the universal
    greeting', *Harvard Gazette*, 30 March 2020, accessed
    8 January 2021, https://news.harvard.edu/gazette/
    story/2020/03/harvard-experts-weigh-in-on-the-fate-
    of-the-handshake/

26. Steve McGaughey, 'Science reveals the power of
    a handshake', University of Illinois at Urbana-
    Champaign, Beckman Institute for Advanced
    Science and Technology, 19 October 2012, accessed
    8 January 2021, https://beckman.illinois.edu/about/
    news/article/2012/10/19/833c5312–07dc-499e-b192–
    941f95db727b

2. Symbolism: What Does the Handshake Mean?

1. As the anthropologist Ethel J. Alpenfels put it, 'man is born with a hand free to do the bidding of his expanded brain'.

2. In *Merriam-Webster.com*, retrieved 8 January 2020, https://www.merriam-webster.com/dictionary/digit#synonyms

3. Ethel J. Alpenfels, 'The anthropology and social significance of the human hand', *Artificial Limbs* 2, 2 (May 1955), pp. 4–21, found at http://www.oandplibrary.org/al/pdf/1955_02_004.pdf

4. Researcher Paul Pettitt and colleagues examined hand motifs in El Castillo and La Garma caves in Cantabria and point to how common it is to see these hands in inconvenient or high-up locations. It's possible they were giving very practical advice and warnings about cave features: many handprints are found around a big well in La Garma cave. It is hard to know exactly what the meaning of the handprints was, just as it is hard to know why so much cave and rock art depicting hands seem to have a missing or shortened finger.

5. Ed Simon, 'When was the first handshake?', *JSTOR Daily*, 26 January 2019, accessed 8 January 2021, https://daily.jstor.org/when-was-first-handshake/

6. 'Origin of hand-shaking', *Coronado Mercury*, 1, 157 (8 November 1887), p. 3, but it is attributed to the *Rochester Post-Express*. However, note that an almost identical quote is attributed to an 1870s issue of *Harper's Weekly* by Sam Roberts, 'Let's (not) shake on it', *New York Times*, 2 May 2020.

7. John Anthony Brinkman, *A Political History*

of *Post-Kassite Babylonia, 1158–722 BC*
(Rome: Pontificium Istitutum Biblicum, 1968).

8. David Oates, 'The excavations at Nimrud (Kalḫu)', *Iraq* 24, 1 (Spring 1962), pp. 1–25, https://doi.org/ 10.2307/4199709

9. John E. Curtis, Henrietta McCall, Dominique Collon and Lamia Al-Gailani Werr (eds), *New Light on Nimrud: Proceedings of the Nimrud Conference 11–13 March 2002* (London: British Institute for the Study of Iraq, in association with the British Museum, 2008); Brinkmann, *A Political History of Post-Kassite Babylonia.*

10. Homer, *The Iliad*, translated by Samuel Butler, Book VI, Digireads.com, 2009, http://classics.mit.edu/ Homer/iliad.6.vi.html

11. Byron Derries, '"Strange meeting": Diomedes and Glaucus in Iliad 6', *Greece and Rome* 40, 2 (1993), pp. 133–46, doi:10.1017/S0017383500022749

12. Janet Burnett Grossman, 'Funerary sculpture', *The Athenian Agora* 35 (2013), pp. iii–246, accessed 3 January 2021, www.jstor.org/stable/26193789

13. G. Davies, 'The significance of the handshake motif in classical funerary art', *American Journal of Archaeology* 89, 4 (1985), pp. 627–40, http://www.jstor. com/stable/504204

14. G. Herman, *Ritualised Friendship and the Greek City* (Cambridge: Cambridge University Press, 2002), pp. 50–52, https://books.google.co.uk/ books?hl=en&lr=&id=bAPk18UKx_MC&oi=fnd& pg=PR9&dq=king+shalmaneser+handshake&ots=SS

wPEvN8ZQ&sig=qWulE52GMNraTs4gKouZiJnVL2I
&redir_esc=y#v=onepage&q=handshake&f=false

15. Davies, 'The significance of the handshake motif in classical funerary art'.

16. Ibid.

17. Ibid.

18. J. Burrow, *Gestures and Looks in Medieval Narrative*, Cambridge Studies in Medieval Literature (Cambridge: Cambridge University Press, 2002), doi:10.1017/CBO9780511483240

19. Ibid.

20. Ibid.

21. Ibid.

22. Dmitri Zakharine, 'Medieval perspectives in Europe: Oral culture and bodily practices', in Cornelia Müller et al. (eds), *Body – Language – Communication: An International Handbook on Multimodality in Human Interaction* (Berlin: De Gruyter Mouton, 2013), p. 347, available under doi:10.1515/9783110261318.343

23. Frans de Waal, *Chimpanzee Politics: Power and Sex Among Apes* (Baltimore: The John Hopkins University Press, 1998), p. 82.

24. Lauren Turner, 'Theresa May and the art of the curtsey', BBC Online, 9 August 2018, https://www.bbc.co.uk/news/uk-45126243

25. Stephen W. Angell, 'The end of the Quaker handshake?', *Friends Journal*, accessed 8 January 2021, https://www.friendsjournal.org/the-end-of-the-quaker-handshake/.

26. Michael Zuckerman, 'Authority in early America: The

decay of deference on the provincial periphery', *Early American Studies* 1, 2 (Fall 2003), p. 12.

27. Jeffry H. Morrison, *The Political Philosophy of George Washington* (Baltimore: The Johns Hopkins University Press, 2009), https://books.google.co.uk/books?id=f3vfS_uxvrQC&printsec=frontcover&dq=the+political+philosophy+of+george+washington&hl=en&sa=X&ved=2ahUKEwiz3tinwsDrAhViWhUIHQ7tAXsQ6AEwAHoECAMQAg#v=onepage&q=the%20political%20philosophy%20of%20george%20washington&f=false p. xiii

28. Conor Cruise O'Brien, 'Thomas Jefferson: Radical and racist', *The Atlantic*, October 1996, accessed 8 January 2021, https://www.theatlantic.com/magazine/archive/1996/10/thomas-jefferson-radical-and-racist/376685/

29. Gottfried Korff and Larry Peterson, 'From brotherly handshake to militant clenched fist: On political metaphors for the worker's hand', *International Labor and Working-Class History* 42 (Fall 1992), pp. 70–81.

30. William F. Chaplin et al., 'Handshaking, gender, personality and first impressions', *Journal of Personality and Social Psychology* 79, 1 (2000), pp. 110–17, https://www.apa.org/pubs/journals/releases/psp791110.pdf

31. The meaning of gestures changes by context, and nuance is important; that same hand kiss is employed by younger individuals to elders in some parts of the world and is a sign of respect in that context, and is also for all intents and purposes gender-neutral.

32. Sheryl N. Hamilton, 'Rituals of intimate legal touch:

Regulating the end-of-game handshake in pandemic culture', *The Senses and Society* 12, 1 (2017), pp. 53–68, https://doi.org/10.1080/17458927.2017.1268821

33. Henry Siddons, *Practical Illustrations of Rhetorical Gesture and Action* (1807), a manual of gestures designed for English actors that was an adaptation of a classic earlier text, *Ideen zu Einer Mimik* (1785), by Johann Jacob Engel of the National Theatre, Berlin.

34. Ibid.

35. Hamilton, 'Rituals of intimate legal touch'.

36. Paul Sendyka and Nicolette Makovicky, 'Transhumant pastoralism in Poland: Contemporary challenges', *Pastoralism*, 8, 5 (2018), pp. 1–14, https://doi.org/10.1186/s13570-017-0112-2

37. Elizabeth Griffiths and Mark Overton, *Farming to Halves: The Hidden History of Sharefarming in England from Medieval to Modern Times* (London: Palgrave Macmillan, 2009).

38. Sheryl N. Hamilton, 'Hands in cont(r)act: The resiliency of business handshakes in pandemic culture', *Canadian Journal of Law & Society* 34, 2 (2019), pp. 343–60, https://doi.org/10.1017/cls.2019.26

39. Megan Garber, 'Good riddance to the handshake', *The Atlantic*, 11 May 2020, accessed 8 January 2021, https://www.theatlantic.com/culture/archive/2020/05/good-riddance-handshake/611404/

40. Edmund Morris, *The Rise of Theodore Roosevelt* (New York: The Modern Library, reprinted edition 2001), p. xxix, https://books.google.co.uk/books?id=u-R37GQsVfgC&printsec=frontcover&dq=the+rise+of+theodore+roosevelt&hl=en&sa=X&ved=2ahUKE

wjDvdm9osHrAhXAXhUIHcVCC4AQuwUwAHoEC
AUQBw#v=onepage&q=lightning%20moment%20
of%20contact&f=false

41. Cara Giaimo, 'The strange world of political
    handshakes', *Atlas Obscura*, 21 October 2016,
    accessed 8 January 2021, https://www.atlasobscura.
    com/articles/the-strange-world-of-political-handshakes

42. Garber, 'Good riddance to the handshake'.

43. Sam Roberts, 'Let's (not) shake on it', *New York
    Times*, 2 May 2020.

3. Finger Snaps and Penis Shakes: Handshakes, Greetings and Cultures

1. Frans de Waal describes a chimp who gave a kiss to
   everyone before leaving in *Are We Smart Enough to
   Know How Smart Animals Are?* (London: Granta,
   2016), while Jane Goodall's impression was that
   chimps don't make a fuss and just leave. See Andy
   Scott, *One Kiss or Two?* (London: Duckworth
   Overlook, 2017).

2. Kerry Wolfe, 'The Ancient Roman cult that continues
   to vex scholars', *Atlas Obscura*, 13 November 2017,
   https://www.atlasobscura.com/articles/mithraic-
   mysteries

3. This would presumably be even more apparent in
   regions with higher population density where the land
   is better (say, nearer the equator) and it would increase
   where borders between groups are more clearly
   defined.

4. Professor Rob Foley in Scott, *One Kiss or Two?*; also

see A. Kendon and A. Ferber, 'A description of some human greetings', in R. P. Michael and J. H. Crook (eds), *Comparative Ethology and Behavior of Primates* (New York: Academic Press, 1973).

5. Rob Foley and Marta Lahr, 'The evolution of the diversity of culture', *Philosophical Transactions of The Royal Society* 366, 1567 (2011), pp. 1080–89.

6. Leila I. Given, 'The bacterial significance of the handshake', *The American Journal of Nursing* 29, 3 (1929), pp. 254–6, https://doi.org/10.2307/3408961

7. K. Dammers, 'Gestures and body language used in public greetings and departures in Addis Ababa', in A. Dohrmann et al. (eds), *Schweifgebiete: Festschrift für Ulrich Braukämper* (Berlin: LIT Verlag, 2010), pp. 60–65, https://books.google.co.uk/books?hl=en&lr= &id=JNdzweB4ksEC&oi=fnd&pg=PA60&dq=han dshake+shoulder+bump+ethiopia&ots=OCPHmx 09uK&sig=aFxJLHIgULcmPVhV2SEspBBsPRg&re dir_esc=y#v=onepage&q&f=false

8. The frequency of *la bise* varies according to multiple factors including familiarity, age, gender and class.

9. Roger S. Bagnall et al. (eds), *The Encyclopedia of Ancient History* (Malden, MA: Wiley-Blackwell, 2013), pp. 3773–5.

10. Preston Phro, 'The importance of "aisatsu" in Japan', *Japan Today*, 9 October 2013, accessed 8 January 2021, https://japantoday.com/category/features/ the-importance-of-aisatsu-in-japan

11. Given, 'The bacterial significance of the handshake'.

12. Larry Powell, Jonathan Amsbary and Mark Hickson, 'The Wai in Thai culture: Greeting, status-marking

and national identity Functions', *Journal of Intercultural Communication* 34 (2014).

13. Irenäus Eibl-Eibesfeldt, *Love and Hate: The Natural History of Behavior Patterns* (New York: Aldine De Gruyter, 1996); and Roth, H. Ling. 'On Salutations', *The Journal of the Anthropological Institute of Great Britain and Ireland* 19 (1890): 164–81, accessed January 30, 2021. doi:10.2307/2842067. It shouldn't be lost on us that presenting buttocks and 'urine washing' are practised by various non-human primates. Realising that these were practised amongst some human populations in the quite recent past is fascinating.

14. M. J. Meggitt, *Desert People: Study of the Walbiri Aborigines of Central Australia* (Chicago: University of Chicago Press, 1971), p. 262.

15. Given, 'The bacterial significance of the handshake'.

16. Richard Darwin Keynes (ed.), *Charles Darwin's Beagle Diary* (Cambridge: Cambridge University Press, revised edition 2001), p. 124, http://darwin-online.org.uk/content/frameset?itemID=F1925&viewtype=text&pageseq=1

17. James Cook, ed. Captain W. J. L. Wharton, *Captain Cook's Journal During the First Voyage Round the World*, Project Gutenberg EBook, last updated August 2012, chapter 3, Tahiti, accessed 8 January 2021, https://www.gutenberg.org/files/8106/8106-h/8106-h.htm#ch3

18. Tim McGirk, 'Islanders running out of isolation: Tim McGirk in the Andaman Islands reports on the fate of the Sentinelese', *Independent*, 10 January 1993.

19. Htwe Htwe Thein, 'Letter from Burma: Obama's awkward kiss', *Guardian*, 11 December 2012, accessed 8 January 2021, https://www.theguardian.com/world/2012/dec/11/letter-from-burma-obama-kiss

20. Yaser Alamoudi, 'Differences in Handshake Perceptions Between American, Japanese, and Saudi Arabia Businesspersons', Masters thesis, Hawaii Pacific University (2010),

21. Derek Sheridan, '"If you greet them, they ignore you": Chinese migrants, (refused) greetings, and the inter-personal ethics of global inequality in Tanzania', *Anthropological Quarterly* 91, 1(2018), pp. 237–65, doi:10.1353/anq.2018.0007. This kind of ethnographic study is quite rare, and this particular example demonstrates that culture may be just one component of greeting confusion; in this case, global material inequalities between China and Africa also played a role.

22. Aurelien Breeden, 'No handshake, no citizenship, French court tells Algerian woman', *New York Times*, 21 April 2018, accessed 8 January 2021, https://www.nytimes.com/2018/04/21/world/europe/handshake-citizenship-france.html

23. Monica C. LaBriola, 'Planting islands: Marshall Islanders shaping land, power, and history', *Journal of Pacific History* 54, 2 (2019), pp. 182–98, doi:10.1080/00223344.2019.1585233 https://doi-org.libproxy.ucl.ac.uk/10.1080/00223344.2019.1585233

24. Jyotsna Kalavar et al., 'Intergenerational differences in perceptions of heritage tourism among the Maasai of Tanzania', *Journal of Cross-Cultural Gerontology* 29

(2014), pp. 53–67, https://link.springer.com/article/10.1 007%2Fs10823–013–9221–6

4. A Step-by-Step Guide to the Handshake

1. 'Firm squeeze and three shakes: Scientists devise formula for the perfect handshake', *Mail Online*, 16 July 2010, accessed 8 January 2021, https://www. dailymail.co.uk/sciencetech/article-1294962/Scientists-perfect-handshake-formula-Firm-squeeze-shakes.html

2. Cari Romm, 'What a handshake smells like', *The Atlantic*, 10 March 2015, https://www.theatlantic.com/ health/archive/2015/03/what-a-handshake-smells-like/ 387325/

3. Angus Trumble, *The Finger: A Handbook* (New York: Farrar, Straus and Giroux, 2010), p. 218.

4. Sheryl N. Hamilton, 'Hands in cont(r)act: The resiliency of business handshakes in pandemic culture', *Canadian Journal of Law & Society* 34, 2 (2019), pp. 343–60, doi:https://doi.org/10.1017/cls.2019.26

5. Ibid.

6. Angus Trumble, *The Finger: A Handbook*, p. 218.

7. Hamilton, 'Hands in cont(r)act'.

8. According to Scouts' lore it comes from an encounter between an 'African tribesman' and the founder of the Scouts, Lord Baden-Powell.

9. Ethel J. Alpenfels, 'The anthropology and social significance of the human hand', *Artifical Limbs* 2, 2 (May 1955), pp. 4–21, http://www.oandplibrary.org/al/ pdf/1955_02_004.pdf

10. Darryl P. Leong et al., 'Prognostic value of grip

strength: Findings from the Prospective Urban Rural Epidemiology (PURE) study', *The Lancet* 386, 9990 (2015), pp. 266–73, https://www.thelancet.com/journals/lancet/article/PIIS0140–6736(14)62000–6/fulltext

11. M. Misiak et al., 'Digit ratio and hand grip strength are associated with male competition outcomes: A study among traditional populations of the Yali and Hadza (2019), https://onlinelibrary.wiley.com/doi/abs/10.1002/ajhb.23321

12. Greg L. Stewart et al., 'Exploring the handshake in employment interviews', *Journal of Applied Psychology* 93, 5 (2008), pp. 1139–46, https://doi.org/10.1037/0021–9010.93.5.1139

13. Hamilton, 'Hands in cont(r)act'.

14. Additionally, the data suggesting a correlation between grip strength and hunting abilities is just a correlation; it is not causation. Might it also be that the better you are at hunting, the more confident you are in asserting some strength in a handshake?

15. Martin Fone, 'Curious questions: How will we greet each other in a post Covid-19 world?', *Country Life*, 18 April 2020, https://www.countrylife.co.uk/comment-opinion/curious-questions-how-will-we-greet-each-other-in-a-post-covid-19-world-214405

5. The Hand of Destiny: History's Best Handshakes

1. Ella Braidwood, '"Gay plague": The vile, horrific and inhumane way the media reported the AIDS crisis', *Pink News*, 3 November 2018, https://www.pinknews.

co.uk/2018/11/30/world-aids-day-1980s-headlines-tabloids/

2. John Phair, 'The antidote for Aids hysteria', *Chicago Tribune*, 3 April 1986, https://www.chicagotribune.com/news/ct-xpm-1986–04–02–8601240358-story.html. https://www.insider.com/photo-princess-diana-shaking-hand-aids-patient-1987–2017–8

3. Interview with John O'Reily, *Witness*, 5 April 2017, footage available at https://www.bbc.co.uk/news/av/magazine-39490507

4. Speech given by Ambassador Pamala Hamamoto at the Reagan–Gorbachev memorial handshake, 31 August 2015, https://geneva.usmission.gov/2015/08/31/handshake-that-changed-history/

5. A photo of this handshake can be viewed at the website of the Library of Congress, accessed 8 January 2021, https://www.loc.gov/pictures/item/2005681248/

6. Barbara Maranzani, 'Martin Luther King Jr and Malcolm X only met once', *Biography*, 12 February 2012, accessed 8 January 2021, https://www.biography.com/news/martin-luther-king-jr-malcolm-x-meeting

7. A photograph of this handshake can be viewed at https://www.smithsonianmag.com/smithsonian-institution/it-time-reassessment-malcolm-x-180968247/; Alison Keyes, 'Is it time for a reassessment of Malcolm X?', *Smithsonian Magazine*, 23 February 2018, accessed 8 January 2021, https://www.smithsonianmag.com/smithsonian-institution/it-time-reassessment-malcolm-x-180968247/

8. Gerry Moriarty, 'McGuinness holds first private meeting with Queen Elizabeth', *Irish Times*, 23 June

2013, accessed 8 January 2021, https://www.irishtimes. com/news/politics/mcguinness-holds-first-private-meeting-with-queen-elizabeth-1.1842706

9.   'Nelson Mandela: Francois Pienaar's memories of Madiba', BBC Sport, 9 December 2013, accessed 8 January 2021, https://www.bbc.co.uk/sport/rugby-union/25305354; David Smith, 'Francois Pienaar: "When the whistle blew, South Africa changed forever"', *Guardian*, 8 December 2013, accessed 8 January 2021, https://www.theguardian.com/world/ 2013/dec/08/nelson-mandela-francois-pienaar-rugby-world-cup

6. The Hand of Doom: History's Worst Handshakes

1.   Serge-Christophe Kolm, 'Reciprocity: Its scope, rationales, and consequences', in S. Kolm and Jean Mercier Ythier (eds), *Handbook on the Economics of Giving, Reciprocity and Altruism* (Amsterdam: Elsevier, 2006), volume 1, chapter 6, pp. 371–541, http://www.vcharite.univ-mrs.fr/idepcms/confidep/ docannexe.php?id=659

2.   Karen S. Cook, 'Social exchange theory', in James D. Wright (ed.), *International Encyclopedia of the Social & Behavioral Sciences* (Amsterdam: Elsevier, second edition 2015), pp. 482–8, https://www.sciencedirect. com/topics/social-sciences/social-exchange-theory

3.   Molly McLeod Mirll, 'Vigorous Cold War handshakes: Reviewing Nixon's 1972 China Trip', Masters thesis, University of Central Oklahoma (2007).

4.   Haley Bracken, 'Was Jesse Owens snubbed by Adolf

Hitler at the Berlin Olympics?', *Britannica*, accessed
8 January 2021, https://www.britannica.com/story/
was-jesse-owens-snubbed-by-adolf-hitler-at-the-berlin-
olympics

5. Tim Ott, 'How Jesse Owens foiled Hitler's plans for
    the 1936 Olympics', *Biography*, 27 December 2018,
    accessed 8 January 2021; 'Seconds that defied Hitler',
    BBC Sportsworld, accessed 8 January 2021, https://
    www.bbc.co.uk/programmes/
    articles/33GFLsLsZb1V3wnJNRKlPjp/10-seconds-
    that-defied-hitler

6. Megan Garber, 'Good riddance to the handshake',
    The Atlantic, 11 May 2020, accessed 8 January 2021,
    https://www.theatlantic.com/culture/archive/2020/05/
    good-riddance-handshake/611404/

7. Douglas Hanks, 'A polite streak broken by Clinton
    and Trump: Looking back at 40 years of handshakes',
    Miami Herald, 20 October 2016, accessed 8 January
    2021, https://www.miamiherald.com/news/politics-
    government/election/article109452062.html

8. Olivia B. Waxman, 'A brief history of handshakes at
    presidential debates', *Time*, 20 October 2016, accessed
    8 January 2021, https://time.com/4538640/handshake-
    presidential-debates/; Cara Giaimo, 'The strange
    world of political handshakes', *Atlas Obscura*, 21
    October 2016, accessed 8 January 2021, https://www.
    atlasobscura.com/articles/the-strange-world-of-
    political-handshakes

9. Jonathan Liew, 'Betrayal and bombast: The surreal
    story of the Terry v Bridge saga', *Guardian*, 3
    May 2020, accessed 8 January 2021, https://www.

theguardian.com/football/2020/may/03/betrayal-and-bombast-surreal-story-terry-v-bridge-scandal

10. Dan Roberts and Jonathan Watts, 'Smiles all around after Obama's Cuba visit – but which side got more out of it?', *Guardian*, 24 March 2016, https://www.theguardian.com/world/2016/mar/24/barack-obama-cuba-visit-raul-castro-analysis; also Giaimo, 'The strange world of political handshakes'.

7. Demise: Is This the End of the Handshake?

1. Nick Paton Walsh, 'There is no getting "back to normal", experts say. The sooner we accept that, the better', CNN, 30 September 2020, https://edition.cnn.com/2020/09/30/health/back-to-normal-bias-wellness/index.html

2. Caroline Davies, 'Elbow-bumps and footshakes: The new coronavirus etiquette', *Guardian*, 3 March 2020, https://www.theguardian.com/world/2020/mar/03/elbow-bumps-and-footshakes-the-new-coronavirus-etiquette

3. Micah Hauser, 'In memoriam: The handshake', *The New Yorker*, 27 April 2020, https://www.newyorker.com/magazine/2020/05/04/in-memoriam-the-handshake

4. Elian Peltier, 'No handshakes, no new citizens', *New York Times*, 7 March 2020, https://www.nytimes.com/2020/03/07/world/europe/denmark-coronavirus-citizenship.html

5. Dan Amira, 'Does Donald Trump have a flesh-pressing problem?', *New York Magazine*, 25 February 2011,

https://nymag.com/intelligencer/2011/02/does_donald_trump_have_a_glad-.html

6. Megan Garber, 'Good riddance to the handshake', *The Atlantic*, 11 May 2020, accessed 8 January 2021, https://www.theatlantic.com/culture/archive/2020/05/good-riddance-handshake/611404/

7. Thucydides, trans. Richard Crawley, *The History of the Peloponnesian War* (Digireads.com, 2017); see also Leonard C. Norkin, *Virology: Molecular Biology and Pathogenesis* (Washington: ASM Press, 2010), section called 'Thucydides and the Plague of Athens', https://norkinvirology.wordpress.com/2014/09/30/thucydides-and-the-plague-of-athens/#:~:text=The%20%E2%80%9CPlague%20of%20Athens%E2%80%9D%20was,reemerging%20there%20in%20425%20B.C.E.&text=The%20Athenian%20historian%2C%20Thucydides%2C%20in,witness%20account%20of%20the%20Plague.

8. Julian Borger, 'Satellite images show Iran has built mass graves amid coronavirus outbreak', *Guardian*, 12 March 2020, https://www.theguardian.com/world/2020/mar/12/coronavirus-iran-mass-graves-qom

9. John M. Barry, *The Great Influenza: The Epic Story of the Deadliest Plague in History* (New York: Viking Penguin, 2004), chapter 29.

10. M. Balinska and C. Rizzo, 'Behavioural responses to influenza pandemics: What do we know?', *PLOS Currents Influenza 1*, 9 September 2009, https://doi.org/10.1371/currents.rrn1037

11. Karen Harvey, *The Kiss in History* (Manchester: Manchester University Press, 2005), p. 198.

12. Connie Jeffrey, 'Social distancing – medieval style: A petition of the Commons in the Parliament of 1439', *The History of Parliament*, 14 April 2020, accessed 8 January 2021, https://thehistoryofparliament.wordpress.com/2020/04/14/social-distancing-medieval-style-a-petition-from-the-commons-in-the-parliament-of-1439/; 'Henry VI: November 1439', in *Parliament Rolls of Medieval England*, ed. Chris Given-Wilson et al. (Woodbridge: Boydell, 2005), *British History Online*, accessed 8 January 2021, http://wwingmpw.british-history.ac.uk/no-series/parliament-rolls-medieval/november-1439

13. Jeffrey, 'Social distancing – medieval style'.

14. Euan C. Roger, '"To be shut up": New evidence for the development of quarantine regulations in early Tudor England', *Social History of Medicine* 33, 4 (November 2020), pp. 1077–96, https://doi.org/10.1093/shm/hkz031

15. Julie Miller, 'The yellow fever epidemic: The Washingtons, Hamilton and Jefferson', *Federal News Feed Library of Congress Blog*, 4 June 2020.

16. Mathew Carey, *A Short Account of the Malignant Fever, lately prevalent in Philadelphia* (Philadelphia: By the author, 4th edition, 1794), p. 23, http://www.usgwarchives.net/pa/philadelphia/history/yellowfever1793.pdf

17. Ibid.

18. Though severe, this epidemic does not compare to those experienced by the Native American populations due to the arrival of European settlers.

19. Herbert L. Fred, 'Banning the handshake from

healthcare settings is not the solution to poor hand hygiene', *Texas Heart Institute Journal* 42, 6 (1 December 2015), pp. 510–11, doi:10.14503/THIJ-15-5254

20. 'Editorial', *Corpuscle* (Rush Medical College), 4, 2 (October 1894), p. 62 (the official organ of the Alumni Association of Rush Medical College, Chicago, Illinois, affiliated with the University of Chicago).

21. 'Annotations', *The Lancet* 144, 3706 (September 1894), pp. 583–90, https://doi.org/10.1016/S0140–6736(01)58938–2

22. 'Spanish Influenza', *Bulletin of the Health Department* (Milwaukee, Wisconsin), October/November 1918, pp. 10–11.

23. Dr H. W. Hill, 'Danger in handshake is seen by physician', *The Circle Banner* (Circle, Montana), 31 October 1919, p. 3.

24. 'Why is a handshake?', *Ohio Health News*, 15 December 1926, p. 3.

25. Owen Gibson, 'London 2012: Team GB athletes advised not to shake hands', *Guardian*, 12 February 2012, https://www.theguardian.com/sport/2012/mar/06/london-2012-team-gb-hands; and 'Olympic athletes reminded to wash their hands', *The Times*, 6 March 2012, https://www.thetimes.co.uk/article/olympic-athletes-reminded-to-wash-their-hands-2sqkcd3bh6f

26. 'The colour of cholera', Médecins Sans Frontières, 3 February 2009, https://www.msf.org/colour-cholera; and James Thompson, 'No handshakes at funerals as cholera spreads in Zimbabwe', *TimesLIVE*, 2

February 2009, https://www.timeslive.co.za/news/
africa/2018–02–02-no-handshakes-at-funerals-as-
cholera-spreads-in-zimbabwe/

27. Sarah L. Edmonds-Wilson et al., 'Review of
human hand microbiome research', *Journal of
Dermatological Science* 80 (October 2015), pp. 3–12,
https://www.sciencedirect.com/science/article/pii/
S0923181115300268

28. Ibid.

29. Leonard A. Mermel, 'Ban the handshake in winter?',
Infection Control & Hospital Epidemiology 40, 6
(June 2019), pp. 699–700.

30. G. Döring et al., 'Distribution and transmission of
Pseudomonas aeruginosa and Burkholderia cepacia
in a hospital ward', *Pediatr Pulmonol* 21, 2 (1996), pp.
90–100.

31. Mermel, 'Ban the handshake in winter?'.

32. J. Reilly et al., 'Are you serious? From fist bumping
to hand hygiene: Considering culture, context and
complexity in infection prevention intervention
research', *Journal of Infection Prevention* 17 (2016),
pp. 29–33, doi:10.1177/1757177415605659

33. N. Pinto-Herrera et al., 'Transfer of methicillin-
resistant Staphylococcus aureus by fist bump versus
handshake', *Infection Control & Hospital
Epidemiology* 41, 8 (2020), p. 963, https://doi.org/10.
1017/ice.2020.192

34. Donald G. McNeil, 'Greetings kill: Primer for a
pandemic', *New York Times*, 12 February 2006,
https://www.nytimes.com/2006/02/12/weekinreview/
greetings-kill-primer-for-a-pandemic.html

35. Anna Gorman, 'Handshake-free zone: Keep those hands – and germs – to yourself in the hospital', *Kaiser Health News*, 30 May 2017, https://khn.org/news/handshake-free-zone-keep-those-hands-and-germs-to-yourself-in-the-hospital/

36. Reilly et al., 'Are you serious?'.

37. S. Kumar et al., 'Handwashing in 51 countries: Analysis of proxy measures of handwashing behavior in multiple indicator cluster surveys and demographic and health surveys, 2010–2013', *American Journal of Tropical Medicine and Hygiene* 97, 2 (2017), pp. 447–59, https://www.ajtmh.org/content/journals/10.4269/ajtmh.16-0445

38. I. C. H. Fung and S. Cairncross, 'How often do you wash your hands? A review of studies of hand-washing practices in the community during and after the SARS outbreak in 2003', *International Journal of Environmental Health Research* 17, 3 (2007), pp. 161–83, doi:10.1080/09603120701254276

39. Anastasia Stephens, 'Hidden germs in our snacks', *Evening Standard*, 4 November 2003, https://www.standard.co.uk/news/hidden-germs-in-our-snacks-7294288.html